CHICAGO DIRT

Deals, Deeds, and Deliverance
An Urban Real Estate Story

Chicago Dirt

Deals, Deeds, and Deliverance
An Urban Real Estate Story

ISBN: 978-0-9912815-0-3

Cover Design / Author Photo John Kutsch

WWW.CHICAGODIRT.ORG

North Development Publishing
107 W. Front St.
Harvard, IL 60033

Printed in the United States

To my wife Marla and son Loren

Nine out of ten millionaires in the United States amass their fortunes in real estate. Real estate might not be as sexy as owning a technology company or a music production studio, but it is the best way to build sustainable wealth. America is rich in real estate. The United States tax code makes real estate the most profitable and protected asset class in this country.

Table of Contents

Introduction

Let me tell you a little secret... serious real estate developers do not write books. Most real estate books on the market are written by good business writers with modest real estate experience. In contrast, my book is loaded with firsthand accounts of my 32 years of business life as I share my experience in an honest, unvarnished fashion. I have loved each moment of my career. Unfortunately, in the summer of 2004, while at the pinnacle of my career, I made an uncharacteristically foolish decision that put my life on hold and landed me in federal prison. Writing this book has been a fulfilling experience, but would never have happened had I not been sentenced to jail.

What follows are stories from my career as a real estate developer in the Greater Chicago Area spanning almost three decades, as well as lessons I have learned along the way. This book is about my successes and failures. The failures, in particular, have been precious learning experiences, as valuable as any of the successes I've experienced. I have always tried to learn from others through their accomplishments and defeats in business. I offer that same opportunity to you; the opportunity to learn from my experiences.

In this book, I highlight the key business and real estate concepts as they appear in each story. This gives you the chance to understand a concept and see exactly how it applied in a real situation. Hopefully, you will enjoy my approach of integrating the accounts of detailed real estate development projects and transactions with conceptual aspects. Some of the best business maneuvers and strategies I have learned have come from reading about how someone else did exactly what I was trying to do. I attribute much of my success to being a great student of history and monitoring trends. History is very good at repeating itself, and savvy investors need to be aware of this in order to position themselves accordingly.

In the epilogue of this book, I share observations on future trends. America and the industrialized world is a volatile environment right now. While predicting the future is a fool's errand, I share some thoughts that may spark your thinking and assist you in making important decisions about real estate - or life!

Part I: A Business Memoir

Chapter 1

Trains, Pop Bottles, and Opportunities

My Formative Years: 1968–1982

I was introduced to the world of real estate and real estate investment at a young age. During my youth, I watched my father locate, purchase, hold, and sell various properties. I found the entire process fascinating, and I knew I wanted to be involved in real estate when I grew up.

I was raised in Highland, Indiana, as the oldest of three children in a Dutch Christian Reformed family. My mother was fourth generation American, and my father was second generation American. My father was a partner in Stannard Power Equipment Company, a business that sold equipment for sewage treatment plants. On the side, my dad would purchase vacant, single-family lots and hold them for resale.

On one memorable occasion, I accompanied my dad to a city zoning committee meeting. He was petitioning the zoning committee to have some of his lots rezoned to allow the construction of duplexes on the property. I was only 12 years old at the time, but I had never experienced anything like that meeting. Many area residents were in attendance to object to the zoning my dad was requesting, concerned that the development of duplexes on these lots would drive down the values of the single-family homes in the neighborhood. My dad's petition for zoning was denied. He later sold the land at a small profit to a single-family homebuilder.

I learned a very important lesson at that meeting regarding the fact that zoning could add value to a property. Had my dad been able to secure the zoning he was seeking, he might have been able to double his money on the lots. As it was, he made a small profit and moved on to his next investment opportunity.

My father continued to invest in real estate, on a small scale, throughout my childhood. I watched my dad make more money part-time from real estate than he did from his day job, his main form of employment. I thought to myself: Why not make real estate my full-time career?

I graduated eighth grade in 1968, the same year that both Martin Luther King, Jr. and Bobby Kennedy were tragically assassinated. The following year, the United States would put a man on the moon. I believe that the very essence of America is displayed through our optimism; the ability to disregard the failure of those two assassinations and, against all odds, expect the success of landing on the moon.

Until the summer of 1968, I had only earned money mowing lawns for a local landlord. However, in June of that year, I was hired for my first real job. I started working at Zandstra Fruit Company, a company in downtown Highland, Indiana that specialized in fresh fruit and vegetable sales. My main responsibility was breaking down 100-pound sacks of potatoes into 5-pound bags and delivering them to the small retail store that was in the front of the warehouse. I earned 50 cents per hour, and I worked 60 hours per week all summer long. Looking back, I am sure the long hours conflicted with child labor laws.

I passed a very busy freight railroad track on my way to and from work every day. As a shortcut, I would walk or ride my bicycle, back and forth, on the path that ran along these railroad tracks. As I traveled along this route, I discovered that the railroad employees riding the train tossed 16-ounce glass pop bottles out into the grass. I knew that each bottle could be returned to the grocery store for a two-cent refund, so I made this my daily route, collecting all the bottles I could along the way. Many times I would find six to ten pop bottles, which gave me an extra 12 to 20 cents per day added to the wages I earned at the fruit company. I also continued to mow lawns, and between all three of my "jobs", I felt I was on top of the world, making more money than I could have ever imagined.

I quit my job at the fruit company in the fall of 1968 to run cross-country in high school, but not before I had made and saved $600. With this money, my father helped me buy twelve shares of General Motors stock at $50.00 per share. Approximately a year-and-a-half later, I sold those shares for $66.00 per share to buy my first car. I was hooked. I fell in love with work and investing, and I always looked for future opportunities to arise. Little did I realize at the time, but before I had even completed high school, my father had introduced me to two of the greatest aspects of my professional life: real estate and investments.

After graduating from high school, my parents expected me to attend a college that was affiliated with the Dutch Christian Reformed Church. Calvin College, located in Grand Rapids, Michigan, was a small school that offered a quality liberal arts education that met their requirements. My dad came up with the idea that I could work during the summer between school years, so I could earn money to help finance my education. If I made enough to cover half of my tuition, he would pay for the other half. That first summer's employment before entering college, turned into an entire year. I postponed my freshman year to work and save money.

While living at home that year, I found a job as a laborer with a construction company. Going into it, I didn't know anything about construction, but I was willing to learn. I eventually worked my way up to a rough carpentry crew that provided framing for new construction homes. When winter rolled around, we were outside framing houses in the freezing cold. The thought occurred to me that I might want to consider enrolling in school that fall. Although brief, the knowledge I gained in that year has proven to be invaluable to my career today.

In the fall of 1973, I began my freshman year at Calvin College. I was interested in business, but the school did not offer any business majors. I ended up majoring in political science and taking the few business courses that were offered. I knew that I wanted to go into business for myself someday. I was sure that I wanted my firm to be involved in real estate; I just didn't know how I was going to get there.

During the summer of 1974, I landed a job driving a garbage truck for Associated Disposal, a small Dutch company in Chicago. It was a very adventurous job for a 19-year-old kid from Highland, Indiana. Until that point, I had not been particularly familiar with Chicago. I had only visited the city on a few occasions although we lived barely 30 miles away. I immediately recognized the opportunity I had to familiarize myself with the city. I went out of my way every day to memorize the street grid. The method might have been a bit unorthodox, but I was able to learn the streets of Chicago like the back of my hand by driving a garbage truck.

I could picture myself working in Chicago one day, and I wanted to discover everything that I could about the city. I quickly learned to identify the good neighborhoods and the bad. I was able to differentiate between the areas I thought had potential and the areas that held no promise. Except for the lakefront areas, I noticed that the city had a lot of run-down buildings and homes in disrepair. The knowledge I gained from that summer on the garbage route has been something I have benefited from for over 30 years, especially in my years as a real estate developer.

I returned to Calvin College in the fall to begin my sophomore year. I began to recognize talents I needed to further develop in order to be successful in business. That year, I really focused on improving my communication skills, knowing that having solid writing and public speaking abilities would be an asset in the professional world. I also spent a lot of time that year cultivating relationships and meeting new people.

The summer before my junior year, I started a small

business enterprise with a college buddy, painting houses in northern Indiana and southern Michigan. I wasn't excited about this venture, since the work itself was extremely mundane at times, and the pay was not very good at all. Still, I tried to take pride in what I was doing and produce quality work. If my name was going to be associated with a project, I wanted to do the best job that I possibly could. This was a maxim that I tried to apply throughout my career.

In 1975—my junior year of college—I was getting anxious. Although Calvin College was a good school, I yearned for a taste of the real world. Halfway through the year, I informed my parents that I needed a break from school, although I did finish out the year. At the time, I couldn't quite understand the purpose of a liberal arts education. That summer, I walked into West Dale Realty, a real estate brokerage in East Grand Rapids, Michigan. I told the manager I was interested in a sales position.

I enrolled in the sales program offered by the brokerage to become a licensed realtor in the state of Michigan. I didn't expect to sell real estate to actual customers, but I wanted the knowledge the sales program provided. The coursework was rigorous; it was more difficult than any class I had taken at Calvin College. After 3 months of preparation, I passed the test. I scored better on the exam than on any of the exams I took in college. Once I immersed myself in the real estate sales program, I knew I had found an area that truly sparked my interest.

After obtaining my realtor's license in the state of Michigan, I turned my attention back to finishing my degree. While I was living in Grand Rapids, I had started looking into transferring to Grand Valley State College. Grand Valley was a bigger school than Calvin College, and it had an agreement with Calvin College which allowed students to take certain courses that weren't offered at Calvin and still earn credit for those classes. I became more interested in the school when I discovered they offered political science majors the opportunity to study abroad in Krakow, Poland. I was also intrigued by another program that was associated with the Michigan State Legislature. This program allowed students to spend a semester working for a state representative in Lansing, Michigan. All things considered, Grand Valley State looked like the best place for me to complete my degree.

I transferred my coursework to Grand Valley in the fall of 1977. My major remained political science. I spent that semester finishing up as many of the required courses for my major. Early in the semester, I inquired about both the foreign exchange program and the program with the state legislature. The application process for the foreign exchange program involved a review of my coursework, writing a few essays, and an interview. I was competing for one of the sixteen spots in the program. I completed the process and waited patiently for their decision. In the meantime, I qualified for the state legislature program, which started the following semester.

In January 1978, I relocated to Lansing, Michigan, and commenced working for State Representative John Engler. At the time, Representative Engler was the youngest elected representative in the history of Michigan. Watching government work from the inside was a fascinating experience—Representative Engler's world was a complicated and chaotic environment. I witnessed the different political interests and power brokers pull at him from every direction. He was a master at putting diverse groups together in a room and coming out with a coherent agreement.

The majority of my time in John Engler's office was used to respond to letters from residents of his state congressional district. It wasn't the most glamorous of jobs, but I was able to fine tune the communication skills I had spent a year focusing on, and the position gave me access to the inner workings of politics at the state level. Most importantly, for both my personal and professional benefit, I was now able to understand politicians from a different perspective.

John Engler went on to become governor of Michigan in the 1990s. After having worked for him, I had discerned that he would be successful in politics. He had intelligence and wisdom that far exceeded his years, and he had a true concern for the welfare of his constituents.

While I was still in Lansing, Grand Valley State notified me that I had been awarded the scholarship to study abroad in Krakow, Poland. After the semester in Lansing concluded, I moved back home with my parents and worked for a construction company in Schererville, Indiana for the summer. I was employed as a non-union carpenter, mainly working on new homes. All I had on my mind was the trip to Poland, so I wasn't really thinking much about the future. I figured I would have plenty of time to get my life together when I returned. Along with the credits I would receive from the semester in Krakow, I would still have one course I would need to complete before graduating.

Before leaving for Poland, I enrolled in an elective science course, as independent study, to fulfill my degree requirements and graduate. In early September, we, the chosen group of sixteen students, left for Krakow. The first three legs of the trip, from Chicago to New York, New York to Copenhagen, and Copenhagen to Warsaw, were uneventful. It was the final leg from Warsaw to Krakow that was more than we bargained for.

Our group was ushered onto a plane that had to be an outcast from World War II. It seemed like it was in pretty bad shape, and it definitely did not look airworthy. The plane was absolutely filthy. The wings were covered with black stains that we assumed must have been caused by the exhaust from the engines. The plane had wires that went from the wings to the tail that appeared to be there for extra support. We could perceive no other mechanical reason for these wires. The plane was not a comforting sight to any of us.

As we moved down the taxiway, the plane shook and bounced all over, even momentarily leaving the ground before getting to the runway. Somehow, those pilots got that plane airborne and 2 hours later, we arrived in Krakow, completely exhausted. Representatives from the University of Krakow were there to meet us at the airport. They had arranged a special dinner and reception for us with a group of students and professors from the university. We learned that the University of Krakow was the second-oldest university in Europe, second only to the University of Prague. The university was started in the early 1300s as a way to immerse students in the sciences and humanities. It was best known for its most famous student, Nicolaus Copernicus, who attended from approximately 1491 to 1494.

Living in Krakow, Poland, in 1978 was a unique opportunity for a group of American college students. The Polish professors truly believed in communism and wanted to convince us of its merits. An often repeated theme in our courses was that upward mobility in America was an illusion that didn't work. I completely disagreed and wanted to debate these topics with our hosts, but one of my Grand Valley State professors would not allow me to ask any questions. He wanted us to refrain from doing anything that could be construed as impolite, since we were serving as student ambassadors representing the United States. I was experiencing the censorship of communism firsthand. The only problem was it wasn't coming from any Polish government official; it was coming from my American professor.

While in Poland, I was able to witness a major historical event for the country. In October, the Archbishop of Krakow, Karol Cardinal Wojtyla, was elected pope. Cardinal Wojtyla took the name John Paul II. This was the first time in over 450 years that a non-Italian was elected pope. Communism did not have much use for religion, although it was permitted by the constitution and never outlawed in Poland. However, the government nevertheless directed their efforts at achieving their goal of an atheistic society. Still, over 90% of Poles considered themselves Catholic. I could see it in the faces of the people in the street: Cardinal Wojtyla's election gave them inspiration and new hope for a better Poland

After returning home, I continued to follow the political news concerning Poland for many years. Pope John Paul II continued to be involved in Poland by supporting the Solidarity movement along with Lech Walesa, which eventually led to the fall of communism in Poland in 1989. In 2006, I returned to Krakow with my wife and son. It was a great chance to revisit the city, to show my family the beautiful architecture, and to visit all the sites I had discovered during my semester abroad. Not much had changed in the city, but it was obvious from all the smiles on their faces that the Poles were much happier under democracy.

I managed to complete my independent study course while I was in Poland. When I returned to the United States, I took the comprehensive exam. After writing a 30-page research paper to receive credit for my semester in Krakow, I fulfilled all of the requirements to graduate. Grand Valley State College awarded me a Bachelor of Arts in Political Science in December of 1978.

Fresh out of school, I now needed to find an actual job. When I began my job search, I soon realized that having a degree in political science was not a great asset in the business world. I had no idea exactly what type of job I could find that utilized my degree. I possessed no delusions that I was going to find employment in government or politics. Instead, I responded to an advertisement I found in the *Chicago Tribune* for a claims adjuster position with Liberty Mutual Insurance.

I interviewed with Liberty Mutual in downtown Chicago in January of 1979. Apparently, they felt I had the makings of an insurance claims adjuster because they gave me the position. I had no prior knowledge of the inner workings of the insurance industry, but luckily that wasn't a major concern for them; they provided a 3-month, intensive, training program.

I accompanied twenty other new hires to the Bismarck Hotel, now the Hotel Allegro, for our corporate training. I endured 90 days of indoctrination into the realm of insurance claims adjusters. When I completed my training, I was assigned to the claims division in Lombard, Illinois. As a requirement of my new job, I had to live within a 10-mile radius of the office. I rented a small one-bedroom apartment about 5 miles away in Downers Grove, Illinois.

On my first day of work, my manager assigned 100 insurance claim cases to me. He wanted me to review them and familiarize myself with the cases. I spent a month speaking with the claimants and updating the files. In a meeting with my supervisor, I suggested that ninety-five of my cases could be settled right away. The last five were beyond my control because they were already in litigation. I was instructed to continue updating the files with any new available information, and I was told not to be so quick to settle. I was new to the insurance business, and it was clear that I didn't know how things worked. It was programmed in my DNA to be efficient and get things done. I wanted to clear my case load as quickly as possible. Obviously, I lacked the mindset required to be a claims adjuster.

By June of 1979, I had quit Liberty Mutual. I had been talking to a college friend, Doug Masolink, about starting a small construction company in Chicago. Doug had been working for Haworth Office Furniture in Holland, Michigan. He was responsible for teaching installation procedures for modular office systems to companies that sold Haworth products. He thought the modular office market would be a great means for us to make a lot of money by installing these systems. Thus, C & D Installations was born.

Modular office systems were the big rage with corporate

America and were just starting to take off. If a company built a building with individual offices, they had to depreciate the cost of the entire building over 39.5 years. With modular office systems, the wall panels and dividers that constitute the system are considered office furniture. Corporations could then depreciate the cost of office furniture over 5 years. This allowed companies to write off these assets quickly, and to save money on construction costs because they didn't need to build individual offices. This was a great tax shelter that many large corporations were taking advantage of in the early 1980s.

My construction experience, coupled with Doug's knowledge of modular office systems, made for a great combination. We became a subcontractor for Haworth Office Furniture. They were looking for union contractors in the United States who could install their systems in newly constructed office buildings. In many urban areas, union affiliation was required to work on any construction site. Often, an installer would be called in to begin an installation on one floor while various union contractors completed work on another. This meant that every installer had to have a union card to set foot on a union construction site.

Doug and I both qualified for union carpenter's cards. Obtaining our union affiliation was a key component in our success. Haworth began sending us small to medium-sized jobs in the Chicago area. Haworth would sell the product, along with the installation, directly to the customer, and we would bill Haworth for our labor to install the systems. Many of the customers were in the Chicago area, but oftentimes Haworth would contact us to do an install in different parts of the country because, at the time, Haworth had not established a nationwide dealer network for their sales and installations.

Some of the Fortune 500 companies we worked with included: Motorola, International Harvester, Atlas Van Lines, Southwestern Bell, and Boston Financial Data Services.

C & D Installations had good years in 1979 and 1980. The modular office system market was doing really well. Jimmy Carter was president, and the nation's economy was dead. We were in a period of stagflation, and Paul Volcker, the Chairman of the Federal Reserve, was trying to combat it with 22% interest rates. Our installation business was booming in the midst of these economic conditions. It proved to be a business that was counter-cyclical to the economy.

In the summer of 1980, Haworth contacted us and asked if we would install their new office system line for Southwestern Bell. The location was a new facility under construction in Omaha, Nebraska. We agreed to the installation without having full knowledge of what we were getting into. We only had four full-time and four part-time union carpenters on our crew, and Haworth had sold approximately 3,000 workstations to Southwestern Bell. We were going to need more manpower than we had to complete this project.

I immediately took a flight to Omaha in order to find local union carpenters for this installation. I had other ongoing projects in the Chicago area, and I couldn't uproot my crew and take them to Nebraska. I met with a representative from the local carpenters' union and explained my needs and the scope of the project. He introduced me to a foreman who would put together a team for the installation. Things seemed to be falling into place nicely.

Haworth had delivered some prototype furniture to Southwestern Bell's new location. I was able to take my new group of carpenters to the facility to assess their ability to learn how to set up and install the modular office systems. I felt comfortable with the team we had assembled. If it weren't for the recession, I may not have had access to such quality labor. The economy was slow, so there were plenty of skilled union carpenters looking for work. I left Omaha with an agreement from the union to hold these men for my use in the coming months.

The installation wasn't due to begin until January 1981. In the meantime, my wife and I had purchased a two-flat building in Elmhurst, Illinois. This was my first foray into real estate. The idea was we would live in one apartment and rent out the other. I had to get my dad to co-sign on the mortgage because I didn't have any credit, and I wasn't taking a regular salary from my business. I drained my checking account by putting a $16,000 down payment on the property. As January rolled around, I did not have the necessary operating cash to finance the installation in Omaha.

I was in a serious predicament. I calculated that I would need $30,000 to get the job started. I had to come up with something fast. I pondered the situation for a while before I came up with a solution. My best option to obtain the money was to call Bruce Weiner, my contact at Haworth, and ask for an advance against our future invoices.

I contacted Bruce and explained to him that our cash flow was very limited because other clients were slow in paying their bills. Due to this, we lacked the necessary operating cash flow to begin the project. I told him we needed a $30,000 advance from Haworth. I had to hold the phone back from my ear as Bruce went ballistic. After a long pause, Bruce instructed me to get my guys started in Omaha. He said to bill them for the $30,000 after the first trucks were unloaded, and he would make sure the invoice was paid that same day.

As the saying goes: Necessity is the mother of invention. I had no cash or credit, but I was able to use my customer as a finance company. I told Bruce how grateful I was and that we could not have started the installation without his help. He wanted assurances that I would never pull a stunt like that on him again. After the cash flow dilemma was solved, the project went very smoothly and was completed at the end of 1981.

Shortly thereafter, Congress passed a law that broke up the Bell Telephone Company nationwide. We ended up having to go back and reinstall the approximately 3,000 workstations, in configurations that met the needs of the new organization. Essentially, we were paid to do the same project twice.

While working with corporate America, I learned several significant lessons. Keep in close communication with to your contact, and be willing to do whatever it takes to solve their problems. If blame needs to be placed, it should always be your fault as the external company, even when it isn't. Protect your contact, help your contact look good to their boss, and they will continue to pay what you ask.

Furthermore, to a large corporation, quality service is more important than price. If a company needs something done at 2 a.m. on Sunday morning, be flexible and agree to do it, and charge them extra for it. Never tell them no. If you follow this wisdom, corporate America will find you, and you will always remain busy.

Finally, a customer who chooses the lowest bid to meet their project specifications will never be satisfied with the contractor they find. The low bid rarely meets reasonable expectations. Avoid customers like this. Look for customers who demand high quality work and service, and the economics will follow.

By 1982, our small company, which started with $100 in a bank account and a 1969 half-ton van, was finally generating some substantial income. I was receiving an annual salary of $75,000, and the company had $260,000 in a money-market account. We had come a long way in 30 months. Although the company was doing very well, I didn't want to increase my salary. Doing so would have required me to pay more in ordinary income taxes. My accountant, Bob Finnigan, suggested that I consider investing in real estate as a tax shelter. He was aware of tax credits available to real estate investors doing historic rehabs in urban areas. I was definitely interested.

Summary

Opportunities in Disguise

The experiences from my early life have provided many valuable opportunities that I have benefited from throughout my career. Being a garbage truck driver, in itself, was not a substantial experience, but it taught me the Chicago street grid. This knowledge has been fundamental when looking for real estate development projects in the city. Likewise, getting a degree in political science did not offer me career options such as becoming a doctor, lawyer, or engineer. My college education, though, was critical to my development as an individual, and it put me in a position to meet my first business partner, Doug Masolink.

A New Worldview

The time I spent working with John Engler, while he was in the Michigan House of Representatives, was essential to my understanding of the political process. It taught me tolerance and patience, which became necessary when I had to regularly endure the zoning process in Chicago. My semester abroad in Poland allowed me to see America through the eyes of the world. It not only made me appreciate what we have here in America, but it also expanded my worldview. I would like to see opportunities to study or volunteer abroad made more available to our young adults. As my professor explained to me, we were student ambassadors for the United States; our young adults would serve as ambassadors, too, showing the world the true American spirit. For me, the experience was life-changing in terms of perspective and maturity.

Take a Chance

Looking back, a major turning point in my life occurred when I quit my job at Liberty Mutual to start my own business. But not everyone supported my decision; my actions were perceived as irresponsible. So many people are afraid to take a chance in their lives. It is hard for someone to walk away from the security that a stable job provides. I took a big risk, and it paid off. Even if I had failed, I would make the same decision again. More than anything else, I learned courage and to think of uncommon ways to change *I cannot do it* into *I can do it*. The difference is only one small word, but the adjustment in attitude was immeasurable to my success in the long run. It is hard to get ahead in life by playing it safe and not taking a chance.

Chapter 2
A True Tax Shelter and the Art of Gang Management
Historic Rehabs: 1983–1986

1901 N. Bissell Street: A seven-unit historic condominium building northeast corner of Wisconsin and Bissell. Rehabbed in 1983.

The Investment Tax Credit was enacted in 1981. It was an initiative pushed by the Reagan administration to help cities like Chicago, Detroit, Cleveland, Pittsburgh, and other northern Rust Belt cities rehabilitate their core. The city of Chicago was a strange mix of highly sophisticated urban office buildings in the downtown area and poor, dilapidated neighborhoods surrounding it. The rich suburbanites would commute daily into the downtown business districts. At 5:00 p.m.—the end of the workday—they would all immediately leave the city and rush back to their suburbs. One business district in particular, the Loop, looked like a ghost town after 5:00 p.m.

Residential housing in the downtown area was limited to the Lakeshore Drive area. Most of these properties were very expensive and not affordable for the typical office worker in Chicago in the 1980s. Any other area, around downtown that offered residential housing, was rundown and simply not safe. Most people who worked in the downtown business districts had to commute, anywhere from 30 minutes to an hour-and-a-half, by car, bus, or train to get to work every day; it was a major inconvenience for many people.

The Historic Sites Division of the Illinois Historic Preservation Agency encouraged investors to rehabilitate historic properties through the use of the Investment Tax Credit. The program provided a 25% tax credit—a dollar-for-dollar reduction in a taxpayer's tax bill—against all the rehabilitation costs on a historic rehab project. However, only the construction costs were eligible for this tax credit, not the original cost of the building. My accountant, Bob Finnigan, explained to me that he thought these projects would be very popular with investors as a tax shelter. I liked the idea and saw the potential for developing a market for residential real estate closer to the downtown area.

Bob recognized my enthusiasm and jumped at the opportunity, suggesting that we create a partnership to try our hand at rehabbing a historical property. To do so, we would both put up a portion of the equity. He would handle the business side of the partnership, given his accounting background and his contacts to raise equity from investors. I was responsible for the construction aspect of the partnership, due to my construction skills and work ethic. This was a very pivotal moment in both of our careers. For Bob, it resulted in the unveiling of his hidden talent for finding investors in our projects. For me, it was my long-awaited entry into the world of real estate.

Our partnership was known as Historic Properties, Inc.

This initial partnership, and the separation of duties, would serve as a blueprint for our careers in real estate development. Our first task was to find a historic district and locate a property within that district to purchase for rehabilitation. At the time, I considered the north side of Chicago as our best chance at success. I drove around the Old Town, Buena Park, and Sheffield districts, all of which had been designated as historic districts. I finally settled on the Sheffield historic district, recognizing the possibilities resulting from its proximity to downtown and DePaul University.

I shared my findings with Bob, and he agreed that we should focus our search in the Sheffield historic district. The district was bordered by Fullerton Avenue to the north, North Avenue to the south, Halsted Street to the east, and Clybourn Street to the west. In the very center of the district, running north and south, was Bissell Street. That is where we found our first historic project; a seven-unit, three story walk-up, located at 1901 North Bissell Street.

We created a separate general partnership specifically for the purchase and rehabilitation of the building. Bob and I each contributed $10,000, and he raised an additional $90,000 of equity from investors. We purchased the property for $200,000, obtaining bank financing to cover the remaining cost of the property and all construction costs.

Our plan was to gut the entire building and rebuild the seven units. The building was an all-brick structure, originally built in 1890. As purchased, similar to other residential buildings in the area, it was in poor condition. No interior walls were salvageable, and the individual units were barely habitable.

Despite this condition, a few tenants resided in the nearly vacant building. Before we could get started on the interior demolition, we had to give notice of eviction to the remaining tenants. It wasn't an easy process, but eventually they all vacated the units within 30 days.

We hired an architectural firm to redesign the seven units as condominiums. Before we could begin, we needed a set of plans to submit to the city in order to obtain a construction permit, as well as approval from the Historic Sites Division. The Historic Sites Division had to sign off on the overall design and the materials that were to be used to ensure that they held true to the original design of the building. Once we obtained both their approval and the construction permit, we got right to work on the demolition.

The entire cost to rehab the building was approximately $500,000. In addition to the interior repair, we also had to replace the roof and tuck-point the mortar joints. The latter process of tuck-pointing the mortar joints was extremely tedious work. It required removing the exposed layer of the mortar between every brick that had deteriorated over the years. When that was finished, the mason replaced all of the mortar and refinished every joint. It was then that I realized it would have been more cost-efficient to demolish the entire building and start over from ground level. But that wasn't the idea behind historical rehabilitation projects in the view of the city; the cost was less important than the history and preserving architecture for future generations.

This was our first project, and we definitely wouldn't have done it without the investment tax credit. That tax credit became our incentive to rehabbing numerous buildings in this district. One of the things that I have always remembered from my economics course in college was that people respond to incentives.

We were preserving the 1890–1920 Victorian architecture for the next 100 years. I had to repeatedly remind myself of this every time I encountered a structural defect in one of these buildings that required creative engineering to overcome. Although owners will always pay more in maintenance costs to rehab a historical building, the underlying motive is to maintain its historic beauty, and certainly, historic rehabs are beautiful when they are completed.

It took us about a year to complete 1901 North Bissell Street. It was very successful for all of our investors. Our tax credit on this project came to approximately $125,000 that was divided proportionately amongst ourselves and the investors. It was a 136% return on invested capital in the form of a tax credit in the first year. The tax credit could have been carried back 3 years, or carried forward 15 years.

One of the stipulations of the tax credit was that the property could not be sold for 5 years. So, after our project was finished, we rented the units to local students and a few brave middle-class folks who believed that the city was coming back and wanted to live in an affordable urban neighborhood.

In 1983, while working at 1901 North Bissell Street, I met a neighborhood developer, Robert Markey, who had been in the DePaul area since the 1970s. The larger DePaul area encompassed the Sheffield historic district, where we had been working. Bob Markey was well-invested in the area by the time we bought our first building; he didn't need the investment tax credit as an incentive to buy urban real estate. Instead, he had believed that the cities were going to come back, and had believed so since the 1970s.

Bob had gone to college and was trained as an engineer. He was also a great student of history and philosophy. One day while sitting on the steps of my property, Bob explained to me that history spanning over thousands of years found the rich and well-educated living in a city's urban core, while the less fortunate were forced to live away from the city, where it was more inconvenient to connect with the commerce and social benefits of urban living. Here we were, sitting in a run-down urban area, and Bob was telling me that the situation was backwards. The wealthy in Chicago had been forced to live outside the city in the suburbs, and the poor essentially controlled the urban core. Recognizing that the city could not be revitalized under such conditions, he was investing money in DePaul, believing that the wealthy would return to the city. Chicago was on the wrong side of history and it would self-correct in the coming decades.

As a suburbanite from Highland, Indiana, who grew up in a new sparkling bungalow, I was blown away by Bob's thoughts. I never considered these concepts in my life. I saw the suburbs as new and upscale, where the streets were always clean. The city was dirty, poor, and crime-infested. To me, this was normal. I can remember many times looking out the windows during the construction on that first project, thinking I was insane. I was constantly second-guessing myself on the purchase of that property. How could this decaying neighborhood ever be a success? Bob's vision of urban revival was the seed of hope that helped me believe that our efforts were not in vain. We could really be a part in the rebirth of this Chicago neighborhood.

As Bob predicted, history prevailed, and the backward living situation in the Chicago area was turned forward. Focused on revitalizing the area back in the 1970s, he had purchased vacant lots in the DePaul area for $3,000 each. He sold those lots 20 years later, in the 1990s, for $200,000 each. Those same lots were sold at prices reaching $1,500,000 at their peak during the 2000s. Even Bob was amazed by this, as his thoughts about history were being validated beyond his wildest dreams.

I have continued my friendship with Bob Markey to this day. He is not the wealthiest businessman I know, but he has the most diligent thinking mind of anyone. Some people think he is eccentric, but I will always see him as the agile young man who had the foresight to buy lots for $3,000 and believe the unbelievable: that the wealthy would return to the city because his studies of history said they would.

* * * * *

935-937-939 W. Armitage Avenue: Historic rehab as the southwest corner of Armitage and Bissell. Rehabbed in 1985

In 1984, Bob Finnigan and I bought our next project, 935-937-939 West Armitage Avenue. We had so much success with our first project that we wanted to duplicate the success with our second. This property was very unique in that 935-937 was one structure, and 939 was a separate structure. That left about an inch between the two buildings. The buildings were located about a block away from our first property on Bissell Street. I had spotted the for-sale signs while we were still finishing up our first project. We received a good deal for purchasing both together because the 939 building had an undesirable trait: it abutted the 'L' train along the entire exterior western wall.

Both buildings were four stories with retail space on the first level. The 935-937 section had three upper levels with four apartments on each level. Our plan was to gut the entire building, leave the lower level as retail space, and rebuild the apartments on the upper levels. As for the 939 building, our plans were uncertain; we weren't sure if anyone would be willing to rent the upper-level space to live in. However, a retail tenant was already in the building when we purchased it, so we agreed to allow the tenant to remain and we did not do any renovations to the lower level.

This construction on 935-937 took about a year to complete. As we were nearing the end, our plans for the 939 building were no more certain than when we began construction.. Finally, I decided that we would leave each upper floor open and add a bathroom and a kitchen. I assumed we could find somebody that would be interested in renting a 3,000-square-foot loft, even though it felt like the 'L' tracks were running right through the middle. Not only could you feel every arrival and departure, but you could also hear every announcement over the loudspeaker. To mitigate some of the problem, I built a sound barrier along the entire western exterior wall that was as thick as two interior walls. I removed all of the windows from that wall and stuffed the barrier with as much insulation as possible. My solution didn't totally fix the problem, but it minimized it to the point that made the space livable. In the end, we had no problem renting the space to adventurous young adults who viewed our notion of a "problem" as a novelty.

My partner, Bob, and I did not put up any equity in our second project. Instead, Bob found an investor for us who contributed $250,000 to the project. Our construction costs for the project were approximately $1,000,000, which gave us $250,000 of investment tax credit. Bob and I were already carrying forward investment tax credit from the previous year. We gave the entire tax credit from this project to our sole investor. He was a cardiovascular surgeon, earning about $1,000,000 of ordinary income per year. That tax credit essentially wiped out his entire tax bill for that year. Needless to say, he was very pleased with the success of the project, and he continued to invest with us for the next 20 years.

Our success continued to roll into our next project, located a few doors down, on the west side of the 'L' tracks, at 957-959 West Armitage Avenue. This time, we had a two-building buffer that reduced the noise from the train. The building was vacant and had been so for years. A local gang had been using some of the space for their illegal enterprises without the owner's permission. This project was definitely a risk, and one we were willing to take. Despite our success in this district, other investors were still reluctant to risk their capital there. People thought that we were crazy to invest in the city; while to us, we were simply capitalizing on opportunities no one else wanted.

957-959 W. Armitage Avenue: Historic rehab at the southeast corner of Armitage and Sheffield. 10 apartments and one 7-Eleven store . Completed in 1985.

This property was a three-level single-structure building with two separate storefronts on the lower level. The two upper levels contained ten total apartments, with five units on each floor.

This was our third building in 3 years. We employed the same formula for this project as we had done previously because it was working so well. I was pleased with the quality of work from our subcontractors, so I saw no need to make any changes. Everything had once again been moving very smoothly, except for one problem: our tools and equipment kept getting stolen from our sites.

It didn't matter how vigilant we were; our supplies kept getting stolen. The neighborhood gangs would literally steal our tools right out from under our noses. I distinctly remember one instance when we were eating lunch on the third floor of 957-959 West Armitage Avenue. I just happened to look out the window and saw a group of kids breaking into one of our vans. Another time, a worker temporarily left a ladder unattended. By the time he returned—one minute later—it was already gone. If we left something on the first floor of a building and went to work on another floor, there was a good chance it would disappear before we got back.

I started to budget a certain amount for theft on every project. After replacing Hilti nail guns, Skil circular saws, and ladders a few times, I talked to Bob Markey to see if he was experiencing the same problems on his job sites. He told me that everybody was having the same problems; it was just one of the risks you took when doing inner-city development. He couldn't believe that I was replacing our stolen tools with new ones. He told me about a place on the south side of town where I could go to try to buy back my tools. I was shocked.

Just south of the University of Illinois at Chicago campus, was an area near Halsted and Maxwell, where a swap meet of sorts was held, generally on Sundays. This was the black market hub of commerce that Bob Markey suggested as a possible destination for our stolen items. I ventured there the Sunday after speaking with Bob, and sure enough, I was able to locate about 90% of our missing tools. I didn't even bother trying to explain that these tools actually belonged to me. It was so cheap just to buy them back. It wasn't worth it to try to negotiate with the proprietor because he was just trying to get his money back out of his investment in the stolen equipment.

Still, buying the tools back wasn't really the long-term solution I was looking for. I needed to come up with a way to prevent our stuff from getting stolen in the first place. I decided to enlist the help of a local fellow who seemed to have his finger on the pulse of the neighborhood. BeeBee was probably in his late twenties or early thirties, I wasn't quite sure. I knew that he had some affiliation with one of the local gangs. He spent his days standing on the corner across the street from my building, drinking a beer from a bottle wrapped in a brown paper bag. Who better to keep an eye on my worksite?

I approached BeeBee and explained my situation. For all I knew, he could have been sending those kids to steal from us. I proposed that I pay him 5 dollars a week—enough to subsidize his drinking habit—to help me put a stop to our theft problem. He was highly motivated by my offer. He assured me that he would take care of the problem. Just like that, nothing was ever stolen from that worksite again. I maintained a friendly rapport with BeeBee during that project. It worked out well having him as an ally.

When we finished renovating the building, we were approached by Southland Corporation, the parent company for 7-Eleven convenience stores. Their agent saw the potential for the Sheffield area, but still wasn't quite sure they were ready to open a store there. In 1985, they did not have any stores in this part of the city, but they were early in their process of identifying locations for new stores. He wanted to discuss our willingness to combine the two storefronts of our building to create a space large enough to accommodate them.

We were thrilled at the prospect of landing such a quality tenant. Normally, we had only been able to find smaller operations for our retail spaces. Our current tenants were signing only one-year leases. Southland Corporation wanted us to commit to a 20-year lease. We had yet to finalize the deal because they still had qualms about committing to this neighborhood. They needed a little time to further research the area to determine if it was a good fit for their store. After over 3 months of market research on the site, they concluded that based on the demographics of the neighborhood and its proximity to the Armitage Avenue 'L' station, enough business could be generated to support a 7-Eleven convenience store.

Southland never would have signed the lease based on the demographics alone. The area was rapidly changing, and no one was sure in which direction it was headed. Rather, the deciding factor for Southland was that the 'L' station had so much pedestrian traffic that would bring thousands of people right past their door every day. They were confident in their marketing to be able to get the people inside. Still, they saw this as a risky move for their business; as he signed the lease, the hand of Southland's agent shook uncontrollably.

Southland quickly converted the space to fit their needs. The store was opened within 4 months. It didn't take long for them to realize that they had hit a home run with this location. Their sales were off the charts, so good, in fact, that their agent contacted me to see if I could find them six other locations near the 'L.' That 7-Eleven location became one of their most successful stores in the country in 1985.

After all of these projects and continued successes, Bob Finnigan and I were starting to see that this inner-city development could be more successful than we had originally believed. I was still maintaining my modular office systems installation business, but I wasn't actively seeking new business. I was constantly busy, and it was becoming difficult to run my business and the rehab projects at the same time. On top of that, I had taken on the responsibility of managing our three properties. When we purchased our fourth property, 2000 North Racine Avenue, I knew that I needed to make a change.

I met with the project manager that worked for my company, C & D Installations. I explained that I was interested in selling my company to him for a percentage of the receivables. He was very eager to take over the reins of the company. It was a perfect opportunity for him, because I was a motivated seller. I was anxious to hand over the responsibilities of the company at a discount, so that I could focus solely on real estate, chomping at the bit to take my career in real estate to the next level.

We bought 2000 North Racine Avenue in late 1985, and the rehab ran through most of 1986. It was a four-story, 50,000-square-foot building, located on the corner of Armitage Avenue and Racine Avenue on the western edge of the Sheffield historic district. The building was zoned M1-2, which would not allow the construction of residential housing. Although it was priced affordably as industrial space, changing the zoning would have doubled the value of the building. I wanted to get this building in our hands as quickly as possible, thinking we wouldn't have any problems with getting the zoning changed. Then again, what did I know? This was the first property that I ever tried to get rezoned.

I hired an architectural firm, Pappageorge Haymes, to create a design for the space. They designed the space for twenty-eight individual condominium units that would require an R-5 residential zoning designation. I hired Greg Furda, a zoning attorney with the Chicago based law firm Sidley Austin, to handle our zoning petition. Before starting the formal process, Greg informed Alderman Marty Oberman that he was representing us, and that we were seeking a zoning change to R-5 residential at our industrial building at 2000 North Racine Avenue. Off the record, Alderman Oberman told Greg that our zoning request was reasonable, but we would first need to hold a community meeting to gauge any opposition to our project.

2000 N. Racine Avenue: 50,000-square-foot loft office historic rehab. Built in 1985.

I met with my architect, and together we prepared for the meeting. We assembled copies of the floor plans and renderings that showed the design of the building's new facade and amenities. This project was almost three times bigger than any of our previous projects. I was excited and proud to be making a positive contribution to the community. I couldn't imagine anyone having a problem with this proposal.

The community meeting was held at St. Joseph's Catholic Church on Armitage Avenue, about a block from our building, and was poorly attended by members of the residential community. However, one of the neighboring manufacturers, Chicago Boiler, was in attendance with a representative from the LEED Council. The LEED Council was a new manufacturing lobbying group whose mission was to preserve manufacturing jobs along the Clybourn and Elston industrial corridor. They objected to our project because it would eliminate a large facility that could be used for manufacturing.

Manufacturing operations had been leaving the city for years. The inferior city buildings had 12 to 13-foot ceiling heights with loading docks that were impossible to navigate for modern trucks. In addition, many railroad and other bridges did not have the clearance necessary to allow freight traffic to pass under. Companies were moving to the suburbs and constructing single-level structures with 24-foot ceilings and state-of-the-art loading docks. These newer facilities were being located with easy access to major thoroughfares. All that were left in the city were mainly antiquated businesses in outdated multi-story facilities. It didn't make sense that the LEED Council was objecting to our project. There were no incentives for a manufacturing operation to move into that area.

Our dreams for the property evaporated before our eyes. Alderman Oberman said that he had to side with manufacturing over condos for twenty-eight yuppies. What we thought was a sure thing turned out to be empty hope. My zoning attorney, Greg Furda, was shocked. I didn't say a word while he talked a mile a minute, telling me that he had made no promises that the zoning would come through. As an attorney, he was just covering his tracks, and I didn't think zoning was a given when I hired him. I knew enough about politics to understand how fickle politicians could be. They will flip-flop on any issue if they think that it is in their personal best interests. Nothing in politics is a given. In this case, I believed that Alderman Oberman had aspirations of higher office, and he probably felt he needed a pro-manufacturing position to help his cause.

We were then forced to develop a plan B for our property. This plan involved working within the existing zoning to create a unique shared office environment. The shared office concept was just starting to become popular in the United States in the 1980s. Our design provided for two retail spaces on the first floor, with separate entrances for the office spaces. The main entrance led to a lobby with access to the upper levels via an elevator or a stairway. The second floor contained thirty-five small offices ranging in size from 100 to 200 square feet each. There were sixteen additional spaces, 1,500 to 2,000 square feet each, on the third and fourth floors. All tenants would have access to a shared conference room and a variety of office services.

When the rezoning didn't happen, we knew that we would have to work quickly to implement the new plan because the Investment Tax Credit was due to expire at the end of 1986. In order for all of our construction costs to be eligible for the tax credit, we would have to complete the project before the end of the year. We worked right up until Christmas, and we managed to get it finished just in time. This was my first industrial building, and I was pleased with the results.

The building became popular with small businesses and entrepreneurs who were just getting off the ground. It provided them with a means of easily expanding their operations as they grew. We had originally planned on building condos, but this concept was working really well.

Then one of the most ridiculous things happened: our neighbor, Chicago Boiler, realized that their industrial building would be worth more if they had it rezoned as residential. They suddenly realized the absurdity of their position a year ago when they were concerned about saving manufacturing jobs in the industrial corridor. Instead, they experienced a revelation. They could make a lot of money if they had their property rezoned, so it could be sold to a residential developer.

I shouldn't have been so surprised. I attended the community meeting to discuss Chicago Boiler's zoning petition. I asked Alderman Oberman how he could support this zoning proposal when, just a year earlier, he denied our proposal. Their site was clearly larger than ours, their property faced Clybourn Avenue, and this rezoning would have a far greater effect on manufacturing in the area than ours would have. Just the year before, he was so passionate about maintaining the industrial purity of the area; now, a year later, he had changed his mind. Alderman Oberman explained to me that if I came to him, he would support residential housing at our site. His offer that day was worthless. He knew I did not want the zoning anymore. We had spent $3.2 million to make our project successful as shared office space.

Politicians and their convoluted policies came and went. I learned that day that, as a developer, I needed to effectively navigate the political world and still create well-planned developments that improved the quality of the community. Chicago was a diverse and dynamic city. As long as we were doing real estate development, our ideas were bound to conflict with ever-changing political interests. Our flexibility was essential to our success. We adopted the following maxim as our motto: Life is all about plan B.

In 1986, the IRS rewrote the whole tax code, changing the rules for the investment tax credit. Under the new rules, the amount of tax credit eligible for redemption each year was limited. It was no longer an attractive strategy for us. The incentive did not exist for us to do any more historic rehabs in the city.

We had completed four projects, one per year from 1983 to 1986. As a part of our partnership agreements with our investors, we agreed to sell each property as soon as we had fulfilled the 5-year holding period that was required to receive the investment tax credit.

The investors on all four projects received at least 100% return on investment in the first year as an investment tax credit. The first three projects generated good cash flow for their 5-year holding periods. We were able to pay handsome returns during that time. When we sold those properties, every investor received at least 250% of their initial investment back. We could not have asked for better results.

The holding period on our fourth project, 2000 North Racine Avenue, expired at the end of 1991 in the middle of a recession. Rents were down, and the building was not generating enough cash flow. We were not in a good position to sell the building. We decided to hold on to the property to see if the market would recover. It was a disappointment that this partnership was not as successful as the others. Still, the investors received their investment back through the tax credits, and probably an additional 30% from the cash flow.

Summary

Look for "Perfect Storms"

At that time, inner-city decaying real estate, plus suburban demand to move into the city, plus the tax credit, created a "perfect storm" for investment success. The Investment Tax Credit helped cities like Chicago transform like no one could have ever dreamed. The amount of tax credit allotted to investors was small in comparison to the countless tangible and intangible improvements to the neighborhoods. The revitalization of the inner city has made Chicago prosper into one of the best big cities in the United States in which to live. The Investment Tax Credit was a tax shelter that offered a financial incentive to preserve, rehabilitate, and/or restore many historic properties, and also revitalized our cities.

Detour Around Obstacles

My failed attempt to get the property at 2000 North Racine Avenue rezoned as residential was an obstacle. It compelled me to seek other uses for the building. The result was a successful shared office building. I converted the misfortune from the situation into a successful opportunity for our investors. It also fulfilled the community demand for much needed office space. I would have never considered this idea had Alderman Oberman approved our initial proposal for residential condominiums. A business problem sometimes is only a small detour on the road to success.

Chapter 3

An Urban Market Comes Alive

Residential For-Sale Development: 1986–1990

Demand for new residential housing in Chicago was rapidly increasing in the late 1980s. Not enough developers were working in the city to meet this demand. Prices were on the way up, and we believed that we were well positioned to be successful in this market. Using the investment tax credit was no longer a part of our strategy. Under our old business model, we would acquire a property, complete the rehab, hold and lease for 5 years, and then sell. Our new business model was much simpler: acquire, develop, and sell.

In 1986, while finishing our final historic rehab, we created a new partnership. The partnership was called America's Offering. We set up this partnership to raise one pool of investor equity, and be able to do multiple development projects concurrently. The entity was structured so that Bob Finnigan and I each would own 25% and the investors would make up the other 50%. A timeline of 5 years was set to return all the investor equity along with any capital gains. The business structure was perfect since we did not plan on leasing any units. We wanted to sell the completed units as fast as we built them.

The first property for our new partnership was brought to us by Rick Hansen of Hansen Realty. I was standing on the loading dock behind 2000 North Racine Avenue when Rick approached me and told me that he had an industrial building located on the western edge of the DePaul area, which I might be interested in buying. We still had a lot of work left to do on our current project, but we wanted to start thinking about our next move. Bob had already raised $1.5 million for the new partnership. The ball was in my court to get a development project started.

Rick explained to me that the building was in a great location, at the southeast corner of Greenview Avenue and

Wrightwood Avenue. He said the building could be demolished, and the property would be perfect for townhomes. My first response was: What's a townhome? Rick laughed at me, knowing I was from the suburbs. We got into his car, and he drove me along Fullerton Avenue between Racine Avenue and Halsted Avenue. Along the south side of the street, Rick pointed out the 20-foot wide and two-and-a-half-story homes that were attached to each other in groups of eight to ten units. We did not have homes like these in the suburbs.

I was always happy when I found a great deal, but this time a great deal found me. Rick had really done his homework on this property, and he just laid it in my lap. He told me the owner was asking $490,000, and we could sign a contract stipulating that the closing was contingent on getting the property rezoned as residential. This building was located right across the street from Wrightwood Park. It was surrounded by residential property, and Rick felt that I would not have any problems getting the zoning. He was confident that the alderman and the neighbors would support a residential development on this site.

I agreed to the seller's price. Once I had the property under contract, I began my due diligence. I never entered the building because I knew we were going to demolish it. This structure was a single-level, 30,000-square-foot warehouse built in the 1920s. Environmental standards had changed so much since 1920 that it was imperative that we have an environmental study completed to ensure that the property was safe for residential housing. Not only was the study crucial, but it was also required for the property to be rezoned from industrial to residential.

In the 1800s, city waste—ashes, horse manure from the streets and stables, food, newspapers, and the like—was generally dumped in areas on the city's edge. My property was one of those locations, as we would discover while constructing the townhomes. Even still, with Chicago's flat terrain, the level of many locations was raised to levels sufficient to support modern city sewers. For this reason, environmental studies were conducted on properties to ensure that rezoning would not pose health concerns.

Luckily for us, the environmental study came back clean. We were ready to move forward with the zoning petition. We worked with our architects, Fitzgerald and Associates, to prepare the plans and renderings to present at the community meeting.

My last experience with zoning was still fresh in my memory. It was only the year before that my proposed zoning change for 2000 North Racine Avenue was rejected at the community level. In addition to my previous experience, I was also mindful of the many hurdles to jump in order to have our rezoning proposal approved.

The zoning process always began at the local level. A proposal has to have the alderman's approval and sufficient community support before it is presented to the zoning committee. An alderman does not have the power to single-handedly guarantee any particular zoning, but he does have the power to prevent it from moving to the next level.

A developer has to present his project to the area residents at a community meeting. All those present are given the opportunity to voice their opinion. No one verifies if the attendees are actual residents in the neighborhood. Everyone in attendance is allowed to vote on the proposal. If one hundred people are in attendance, all one hundred people will vote. If there are only twenty people there, then only twenty people vote. It is true democracy at its finest; everyone has a voice. That could go either way for a developer trying to get his zoning approved.

If a zoning proposal is not approved at the community level, the proposal is dead. It goes no further. If the proposal passes at the community level, then it is presented to the city zoning committee by the developer at the zoning committee meeting. The seven aldermen then have the opportunity to question the developer before they vote on the proposal. The committee can table a proposal if they require more information to make their decision. If the proposal does not get approved by the zoning committee, the proposal dies there. If approved, on the other hand, the proposal is then scheduled for a vote at the next city council meeting.

When a zoning petition reaches the city council, no further presentation is required. The petition is simply placed on the city council's agenda. The city council is made up of all fifty aldermen and the mayor (or vice-mayor), who serves as the chairman. When an item on the agenda comes up for a vote, all fifty aldermen will vote on the issue. The chairman only votes when there is a tie. When a zoning change is approved by the city council, the actual zoning does not take effect until the next meeting, when it is officially recorded.

Marty Oberman was no longer the alderman for DePaul. The new alderman was Edwin Eisendrath. We contacted Alderman Eisendrath and explained that we had an industrial site in his ward that we wanted rezoned for residential housing. He arranged for us to hold a community meeting to present our proposal. The meeting was held at the Christopher House, a local learning center about a block from the site. Alderman Eisendrath was not in attendance; instead, his assistant conducted the meeting. After our presentation, the floor was opened to members of the community. Several people spoke negatively about the project concept. Home values in the neighborhood ranged from $75,000 to $150,000. Our development would offer new townhomes for $200,000 to $250,000, which, as a result, would surely raise the surrounding home values. There had been no new development in the area since the 1950s. I did not understand the resistance we were getting from the community. I remembered from my attempt to get our property rezoned at 2000 North Racine Avenue that there are no guarantees when it comes to zoning. This one was supposed to be easy.

The meeting was not going very well. Things were

winding down, and they were getting ready to vote on our petition. It did not look good for our project. Then a miracle happened. A man in his twenties stood up and addressed those in attendance. I had no idea who this man was, and I had no idea what he was about to say.

This young man explained how he could not believe what he was hearing. He said that instead of complaining, the community should thank us for coming to their neighborhood and spending our money to improve it. The development would be like a "pot of gold" for the area homeowners. All the homes would go up in value, and if they were not happy, they could sell their homes and move away. I sat there shocked. Where did this guy come from? Why did he wait so long to speak up?

I was very grateful for what this man said. I could have stood up front and said the exact same thing, but it wouldn't have made a difference; hearing it from someone in the community made all the difference. There was an elderly woman who made a final comment before the vote, voicing her fear that home values would in fact rise and consequently, property taxes would rise as well. She could not afford higher taxes, and she did not want to sell her house and move to a different neighborhood. These were legitimate concerns, but I did not have an answer for her. It was a very delicate situation.

When they finally took the vote, our proposal passed without difficulty. We were very pleased with the outcome, and from that day forward, we referred to that man's speech as "The Pot of Gold Speech."

A community that becomes anti-development becomes static. There were a lot of people like this elderly woman who would have been happy with no changes to the community. But that is not good for the community. Without intelligent development, a community will decay as both the structures and the population ages. New families will avoid the area because it will lack the amenities they require. These are the young families that are necessary to perpetually carry a neighborhood forward into the future.

I agreed with the elderly woman. The increase in her property taxes might make her unable to afford to live in her home. Nevertheless, to impede growth and change with the future was a penalty to every citizen in the neighborhood. They could benefit from new growth and development. Eventually, politicians recognized this unintended consequence of skyrocketing real estate values. Seniors living on fixed incomes became eligible to have their property taxes frozen, allowing them to stay in their homes without any changes in their tax bill.

The new zoning on the property was R-4 residential, which permitted us to build one unit on every 900 square feet of dirt. The standard lot size for our development was 20 feet by 45 feet, and the footprint of the townhome was 20 feet by 30 feet. This left 300 square feet for a small front yard. The plans called for twenty-three townhomes, 1,800 to 2,200 square feet each, and six 1,200-square-foot condominiums on a non-contiguous parcel. We called the development Wrightwood Court Townhomes.

The demolition of the existing structure began in September 1986, at which time we had two projects in different stages of development. I continued to work as the general contractor for all of our projects. In an effort to keep our expenses down, I did not take a salary, and all construction was billed at cost to the partnership. I would get paid my share of the profits along with the other investors.

Once the demolition was completed, we laid the foundations and started construction. The investor equity was used to purchase the property, and a line of credit was established to finance the construction. We employed a few different subcontractors than we had in our previous projects because of the nature of the project; this was our first new-construction development, while all our previous projects had all been rehabilitations. Our plumbing, electrical, and

HVAC subcontractors all remained the same. We continued to stay with what was working. Their businesses were growing right alongside our business. For every project, we would solicit three competitive bids, and the same subcontractors would submit the best bids to us because they wanted to continue to work for us.

Southeast corner of **Wrightwood Avenue and Greenview Avenue**.
Wrightwood Court Townhomes / 29 units in two buildings.

The construction on the townhomes was conducted in two phases, allowing us to minimize our financing costs by selling some of the completed townhomes before starting on the next phase of construction. By doing this, our outstanding line of credit never exceeded half of the total cost of the project. We paid down the debt as we sold units, and borrowed the money back as it was needed. This became a financing strategy we would use often on future projects.

It took about 18 months to finish the entire development. The finished product was a Victorian-style, three-story townhome with a brick facade. Each home had two bedrooms, a full bath, and two half baths. Every unit had a family room and a garage on the first level; a kitchen, living room, and dining room on the second; and two bedrooms on the third. The larger units, which were on the corners of the development, had an additional bedroom on the third level. These homes were very popular, and we had no difficulty selling them. A townhome in Wrightwood Court that sold for $225,000 in 1987, sells for $500,000 today.

During the second phase of construction at Wrightwood Court, I was introduced to Harold Zakharov by Rick Hansen of Hansen Realty. Harold managed a trust that owned millions of square feet of multi-story industrial buildings, mostly in Chicago. After World War II, Harold's four uncles purchased as much industrial real estate as they could. When they died, the properties were left in a trust for their widows. Harold now spent his life liquidating these assets. One of the properties in the trust was a 250,000-square-foot four-level building located at 1800 West Roscoe Street

1800 W. Roscoe Street: Roscoe Village Lofts. Designed and rezoned in 1988, and resold in 1989 to Tom Snitzer and Marshall Bennett. Rehabbed in 1990.

Harold was willing to sell the building for $1.25 million, which was $5 per square foot. This was a fantastic price, but it came with a few problems: the building was zoned industrial, there was a tenant in place with 2 years left on the lease, the same tenant was paying below-market rent, and the City of Chicago Water Department had a lien on the property for a $135,000 unpaid water bill. Solving these problems was the key to adding value to this purchase. Other buyers were staying away from this building because they did not know how to solve these problems, or they were unwilling to do so. I agreed to purchase the building for our partnership, America's Offering, confident I could add value to this property by solving these problems.

I believed I could handle the first problem, the rezoning issue. The building was zoned industrial, and if we wanted to use the property for residential development, it had to be rezoned. After my two zoning experiences, I was one for two. Fifty percent is not so bad in Chicago.

The building was located in a residential area, and the neighborhood considered it an eyesore. Cleaning it up and turning it into residential housing would provide a great lift to the community. I spoke with a few members of the community and got the general impression that the neighborhood would support our development. Zoning seemed like an easy problem to fix.

This time around, we decided we would not demolish the building. The way it was originally designed, we could turn it into a complex of loft condominiums. Our architects, Fitzgerald and Associates, designed 180 individual units ranging in size from 600 square feet to 1,500 square feet. The Alderman for Roscoe Village, Eugene Schulter, supported the plan. He arranged a community meeting at a local church for us to present our proposal to the neighborhood residents. The meeting was almost 2 hours long. The residents complained about problems our development might create, but in the end, all 107 people from the community present voted to approve our zoning.

That night, in the back of the room, was a small group of real estate brokers. They were keeping a close eye on our project. It is a known real estate strategy to follow larger development projects closely because they can have an immediate effect on property values. The day after our zoning was approved by the community, brokers and smaller developers were buying up properties in the area. They were taking advantage of the low prices before the local market had a chance to adjust. They knew that once our development got started, the area real estate would instantly become more valuable.

Our petition for zoning still had to make its way through the zoning committee and the city council before we could begin. There was no real hurry because we had a tenant who had a lease that did not expire until 1989. The tenant was a medical supply manufacturer called Smith and Nephew MPL of London, England, that made hypodermic syringes. As a result of the nature of their business, their office would occasionally be broken into and their inventory raided to supply clean needles to the local intravenous drug users.

We informed the company that their lease would not be renewed upon expiration. We were actually losing money every month because their rent was set at below-market rates. There was nothing I could do; we just had to wait out their lease. I decided I could use this time to resolve the second issue associated with this property, the lien situation with the City of Chicago Water Department.

The lien was for an unpaid water bill in the amount of $135,000. That was a lot of money in 1987, and it was really a lot of money for a water bill. This was Chicago, located next to the largest source of fresh water in the world: the Great Lakes. Water was cheap. I couldn't imagine how many gallons of water would have to be used to have a $135,000 water bill. Why did no one else see a problem here? The lien transferred with the property. If I wanted to sell individual residential units, I would have to fix the problem, or the lien would be attached to every title.

The easy solution was to pay the bill, effectively removing the lien. But I believed I could at least negotiate the amount down. I wasn't too eager to pay a $135,000 water bill, but I also was not going to let it get in the way of our development.

Water bills are calculated by taking the number of gallons used and multiplying by the rate per gallon. The number of gallons used is determined by a reading of the water meter located on the property. If a customer believed their water bill was calculated incorrectly, it could only be one of a few problems. It could be that the meter was not working properly, the meter reader was not reading the meter correctly, or there was an unknown water leak on the property. After discussing the situation with my construction manager, Jim Ridley, we drove over to the property to take a look at the water meter.

The water meter was located on the first floor, on the inside of the building. Jim took one look at it and noticed that it was different from the one he had at his house. The one he had at his house had four digits to the left of the decimal point and this one had only three. I went to the water department to find out if there was a difference between residential and industrial water meters. There was no difference; however, new water meters had four digits, whereas old ones had only three. The water department was unaware of any old water meters still in use. After the 1950s, old meters were no longer installed. But our building was built in the 1920s; it had an old water meter.

I went to bed that night contemplating the outstanding water bill. At 4:00 a.m. that morning, I jumped out of bed; I had the solution. It had been staring me right in the face: the bill was off by a factor of ten. Instead of $135,000, the bill should have been $13,500. I assumed the meter reader had added an extra zero by accident. They were probably accustomed to reading the new meters and simply made a mistake by misreading the old one.

I contacted a supervisor at the water department, and I quickly brought him up to date on my dilemma. He agreed to come to the building to inspect the water meter. After seeing the old meter, he immediately understood the problem. The next week, we received a revised bill in the mail for $13,500. I spoke with our tenant and showed them the new bill. They agreed to pay the entire amount because it was more in line with their actual usage.

In 1989, as the lease was ending at 1800 West Roscoe Street, Tom Snitzer, another developer, approached me about buying the property. I had spent about a year getting the zoning and removing the lien from the title. We had paid $1.25 million for the property less than 2 years before. He offered $3.5 million to purchase the building. I agreed to the sale with the condition that he would agree to use our design that had been approved by a neighborhood advisory group, specially created by Alderman Schulter for our project. I did not think that the alderman would have a problem with the transaction if Tom Snitzer kept our original design.

I was wrong. When Alderman Schulter found out that we were flipping the property to Tom Snitzer, he was *livid.* However, there was nothing he could do to prevent the sale, and I could not turn down the offer. It was a great opportunity for our partnership to make $2 million. We had made no improvements to the property. The added value came from the zoning change, clearing the lien from the title, and the increased market demand. We took risks where others were unwilling to do so, and it paid off.

Tom Snitzer did a wonderful job on the development. He stayed true to the design, exactly as agreed upon. He initially rented the units as apartments, but years later they were sold as condominiums. Today, the development is still known as the Roscoe Village Lofts. If you look at any of the cornerstones of the building, you will see terra cotta pencil points inset in the limestone. This was a design element of the original owner, the Eversharp Pencil Company.

Just as we were finishing up at Wrightwood Court, my architect, Pat Fitzgerald, contacted me about another project. Pat had already designed a townhome project at 2100 West Balmoral Avenue, across from the Rosehill Cemetery. The project was being called Balmoral Court Townhomes. The community had lost confidence in the current developer's ability to complete the project to their standards, and the alderman, Pat O'Connor, wanted another developer to take over this project. Since Pat Fitzgerald had designed Wrightwood Court Townhomes and Roscoe Village Lofts for me, it was only natural for him to suggest me as a replacement developer for this project.

We met with Alderman O'Connor at 7:00 a.m. at a cafe that was not yet open that day for business. Alderman O'Connor walked straight into the restaurant, came right up to me, pointed his finger and said, "You developers do me no good. I am going to let you buy this project from the other developer that the community does not like. And I will let you do this deal, but if you screw up, I will be all over you." With that, he turned around and walked out of the restaurant. I thought he would at least to sit down for a cup of coffee.

We purchased the Balmoral Court project for our partnership, America's Offering. The property had a 40,000-square-foot greenhouse that was still standing. The plan was to demolish the structure and build forty townhomes on the site. I had no input in the design because it was part of the package deal. We bought the property from the other developer at his cost.

Before we had a chance to start the demolition, I found out from my attorney that we were being sued. I had only owned the property for 10 days, but, in that time span, a 12-year-old boy had broken into the greenhouse and twisted his ankle on our property. The lawsuit went to our attorney first because he was listed as our registered agent on the property's title. Our attorney then contacted me, and I, in turn, contacted our insurance carrier. I discussed our options with them. I did not want the insurance company to settle the claim. I actually wanted to have the kid arrested for breaking and entering, and trespassing. The claims adjuster discouraged me, believing that the boy's arrest would only further inflame the situation. The family of the boy pressed us for about a year, but we never settled. They were hoping the insurance company would eventually give in. We knew their lawsuit lacked merit, and would never see the inside of a courtroom. We moved forward with our project, and eventually they gave up pursuing the lawsuit.

2100 W. Balmoral Avenue: Balmoral Court Townhomes.
40-townhomes built in 1989 in the Lincoln Square neighborhood.

We finished the Balmoral Courts development in the spring of 1990. The units took a little longer to sell than we expected. The housing market had been slowing down since the middle of 1989. Our development consisted of forty mostly identical units at the same price point. The only variation was that the corner units were more coveted and sold for $159,995, instead of the regular price of $149,995. The lack of variety made it more difficult to sell the units, but we had been encumbered by the design of the development that had already been approved when we took over the project from the other developer.

Alderman O'Connor was pleased with the completed project at Balmoral Courts. We kept our end of the deal, and, in the process, I think I gained his respect. In 1990, after the final unit was sold, we began wrapping up operations for our America's Offering partnership. We disbursed all of the profits to our investors, along with their initial investments. With the real estate market slowing down, it seemed like a good idea to take a break from any major development projects until conditions improved.

One of the things I learned during this time was that we were giving our architects too much autonomy. They may not have realized it, but they were dictating the marketing strategy for a project through a design. Developers relied on the expertise of the architects to determine the square footage of the individual units within a development. The square footage was then used to determine the respective price points for the condominiums or townhomes. I realized I needed to reverse this process, so I could have more control over the unit size and the overall project design. To do this, I needed to study the market and see what price points were affordable for the income levels of an area where we planned to develop. I would then need to select unit sizes based on these price points and have the architects create designs to fit our requirements. No longer would I give architects free rein to control the design of a project and set the price points for the completed units.

Summary

Follow Market Demand

The Investment Tax Credit demonstrated that if we renovated historic buildings and developed upscale residential housing in the city, the suburban professionals would move into this market. We would've never done those projects without the tax credit, but once the market became established, the opportunities became attractive without the tax credit. When the tax code was rewritten in 1986, the rules for the Investment Tax Credit were modified, and it was no longer as effective as a tax shelter. The next step for us was to move from doing historic rehabs to hold as rental units, to building condominiums and townhomes for resale. The market was telling us that the demand was there. As long as we kept building, the buyers kept coming.

Zoning Adds Value

It became obvious how indispensable zoning was in adding value to a property. In all cases—Wrightwood Court, Roscoe Village Lofts, and Balmoral Court—the zoning had to be changed from manufacturing to residential. This was a reversal in trends. In the 1950s, the City of Chicago had rezoned vast areas of the city from residential to manufacturing. They envisioned extensive growth in factories that never occurred on the scale that was expected. By the 1980s, manufacturing was stagnant in the city, and it was recognized by most neighborhoods that new development was key to urban renewal. As a result, builders and developers were now required to rezone a property before moving forward with a residential development. The biggest challenges we faced involved convincing those that didn't see new development as beneficial, that it was truly good for their community—the projects that received rezoning created value not only for the developers, but also for the community. To this day, the sites that did not receive this rezoning remain vacant or underutilized. The clash between the demand for upscale urban residential housing, and the City of Chicago Planning Department's focus on preserving manufacturing districts, became a reoccurring theme and obstacle in my business life.

Adversity Breeds Creativity

In the course of business, the problems and challenges I have faced have taught me to analyze situations from various perspectives and to develop the best solutions. Each challenge that I was able to overcome prepared me to handle more diverse situations in the future. In my line of work, the hurdles sometimes seem endless. I have spent years learning how to jump these hurdles, so that now many challenges are simply routine. Some of the best ideas are the result of creativity in moments of adversity. Staying calm and not panicking allows creative thought to surface in reaching solutions to difficult problems.

Chapter 4

Bankruptcy, Mortgages, and Justice

The Elks Club: 1987–1989

In August of 1987, a broker contacted me about a property he thought I might be interested in. I was in the middle of the Wrightwood Court project, and I had just purchased the property at 1800 West Roscoe Street. All of our capital from the America's Offering partnership was tied up in our other projects. But I was still interested in acquiring other properties on my own for investment purposes, or for future development projects. There was not much of a downside to taking a look at the property to see if it was something that was worth buying. The property was located in Rogers Park. It was a former Elks Club that had fallen on hard times. The site was approximately 2 acres, and it contained a large single-room building.

1925 W. Thome Avenue: Former Elks Club, Unity Church property rehabbed in 1989 by Unity Church.

When the broker showed me the property, I realized the location alone had plenty of potential. I knew if I purchased this property, I could demolish the existing structure and develop affordable single-family homes or townhomes. I offered to buy the property for $550,000. This amount would allow me to develop homes at a price point competitive in the Rogers Park neighborhood and still make a nice profit. The Elks Club accepted my offer and agreed to a November closing date.

I was a little short of cash because it was all tied up in other projects, and there was no capital available in our partnership. If I wanted to do this deal, I had to find a partner to help me. I got in touch with a fellow developer named Howard Robinson. Howard was intrigued by the deal and agreed to the partnership. After signing a partnership agreement, Howard took off for Spain and left me to take care of business. The partnership provided me with sufficient capital for the earnest money and down payment. Now, all I had to do was work on getting a mortgage in place before the closing date.

A few weeks later, Jerry Olson of Hansen Realty contacted me. He knew I had a contract on the Elks Club, and he had already found a potential buyer. The buyer was a small church, Unity Church, looking for a location to accommodate their growing congregation. I agreed to let Jerry show them the property. The representatives from the Unity Church were impressed. The property fit their needs, and they could use the existing structure with little renovation. Jerry called me right away, said that they were interested in the property, and wanted to know what my asking price was.

This was a new situation for me. I had a potential buyer ready to make an offer on a building that I didn't even own. I hadn't planned on selling the property, but plans change. If I could work out the details, I could close on the deal with the Elks Club, then flip it to Unity Church. I stood to make a handsome profit with little effort. I contacted my attorney,

Joe Palmisano, to run the deal by him. He didn't see a problem with it. He determined the only exposure to risk I had would surface if I failed to deliver the property to Unity Church on schedule. I felt the potential of this deal was worth the risk.

I called Jerry back and told him I would accept $950,000 for the property. Unity Church agreed to the price, and we signed a contract with a February 1988 closing date. My plan was to secure financing, close with the Elks in November, and hold the property until February for Unity Church. I didn't see anything that could jeopardize the deal. The plan seemed solid.

In late September, I was able to arrange financing, and everything was in place for our closing with the Elks Club. At an early October meeting with my partner, Howard, and my attorney, Joe, Howard suggested that we could complete the closings back to back. First, we would have to get the Elks Club to agree to back up the closing date to the same day we closed with Unity Church in February. Then, we had to contact the title company to let them know what we wanted to do. We would use the proceeds from the Unity Church closing, literally walk to another room at the title company, and close with the Elks Club. This would save us from having to pay the costs associated with the mortgage, property taxes, insurance, and utilities for the period that we owned the building until the closing with Unity Church. If we did this, the title would remain in limbo until the closing with the Elks Club. Unity Church would have to wait at least an hour to receive a warranty deed from the title company. This would allow us plenty of time to close with the Elks and clear the title.

Both Howard and Joe were in agreement that this was a great idea. I reminded them that I already had financing in place, and we were on schedule to close in November. Ultimately, I deferred to their experience and went along with this plan. We contacted the Elks and they agreed to back up the closing date to February. In exchange, we agreed to terminate our due diligence period, which would forfeit our right to recover the earnest money that was held in escrow.

Weeks went by with no problems. Then in January, my attorney got a call from the Elks Club. They were filing Chapter 7. Joe was stunned; he knew immediately that Chapter 7 bankruptcy would give the Elks Club the option of whether they wanted to honor our contract or not. Joe later called me with the bad news. I didn't know where we went wrong with the deal.

As the events unfolded, we determined that Unity Church had innocently contacted the Elks Club looking for a set of plans for the property. The Elks Club quickly learned that the same building that I was buying from them for $550,000, I was selling to Unity Church for $950,000. The attorneys for the Elks Club knew that if they filed for Chapter 7 bankruptcy, then they wouldn't have to honor my contract, and subsequently could sell their property directly to Unity Church. It was a brilliant move on their part.

I went home that Friday, not having a clue as to what I was going to do. We couldn't find any legal means of forcing the Elks Club into honoring the contract. They were protected by the bankruptcy laws. Over the weekend, I just happened to run across an article in the paper about how Sam Zell acquired a multi-million dollar office tower in Salt Lake City, Utah. Sam Zell was one of the most successful real estate investors in the world. The article explained how he was competing with three other real estate companies to purchase this property where the owner was in default on the mortgage. While the three other companies were in negotiations directly with the buyer, Zell simply contacted the bank and inquired about purchasing the mortgage. The bank was excited to dump the loan and gladly sold the note to Zell. Zell then proceeded to foreclose on the property, and cut out the other three companies that were trying to buy the office tower. Zell's maneuver was simply genius.

If this strategy could work for Zell on his multi-million dollar acquisition, there was a possibility that the same strategy would work for me. I thought about the situation over the weekend, then immediately went to see my attorney first thing Monday morning. I asked Joe if he knew if the Elks Club had a mortgage on their property. I told him that if they had a mortgage that I wanted to buy the mortgage from the bank and then foreclose on them. He dropped everything he was doing and got straight to work.

Joe contacted the title company and found out that the Elks did indeed have a mortgage, and it was held by Uptown Savings and Loan. Since the Elks had filed for bankruptcy, we assumed that they were in default on their mortgage. Joe then contacted Uptown Savings and Loan and spoke directly with the loan officer in charge of the Elks Club mortgage. The loan officer verified that the Elks Club had a mortgage with a balance of $150,000 that was currently in default. After further inquiry, Joe revealed that the bank would be willing to sell the mortgage for 100% of the loan amount in default.

I only had $75,000 in the bank, and I needed $150,000 to buy the mortgage. I tried to contact my partner, Howard Robinson, but again he was unavailable and out of the country. My only option was to call my father. I explained the deal to my dad, and he agreed to partner with me and put up the other $75,000 to buy the mortgage.

We had the money within 2 hours, and were at Uptown Savings and Loan buying the mortgage. Shortly thereafter, I called Unity Church to let them know that we were still on schedule for our February closing.

When Howard returned from vacation, I brought him up to date on what had transpired while he was gone. He was a little nervous that he had lost his partnership interest when the Elks Club filed bankruptcy. He didn't know if he was still a part of the deal since it had radically changed, and I had brought my father on as an additional partner. I assured him that he was still my partner, but that we would have to reserve a percentage of the profit for my father's contribution.

We then discovered that the Elks Club was 2 years delinquent on their real estate taxes in the amount of $75,000. By purchasing the mortgage, we had legal standing to redeem the past due amount for the taxes. I discussed the situation with Howard, and we both saw this as another step that we could take in securing our interest in the property. Howard and I both agreed to split the cost for the tax bill.

The original contract price on the deal was $550,000. We paid $150,000 to buy the mortgage from the bank and $75,000 for the back taxes. We then had control of the property for $225,000, less than half of the original contract price. In discussions with Joe, he advised that we should offer the Elks Club the opportunity to honor the original contract. Joe's thinking was that while we stood to make an extra $325,000 on the deal, we might end up spending more than that in litigation fees if the Elks decided to sue. I agreed with Joe, wanting to get this deal closed, then put it all behind me. I definitely didn't want a lawsuit lingering over my head for years. Joe contacted the attorneys for the Elks Club and gave them our proposal. They weren't interested. I didn't know what their next move was, but ours was to foreclose on the property.

The foreclosure proceedings had to be conducted according to the rules in the Uniform Commercial Code because the property was considered commercial property. The rules required us to give notice to the debtor that we were commencing foreclosure proceedings. We were also required to advertise for 3 consecutive weeks a notice of public auction where any interested party could bid on the purchase of the mortgage. We advertised our notice in the Chicago Law Review that the auction would be held on January 22, 1988 at the law offices of Joseph Palmisano & Associates.

No one showed up on the day of the auction. The Elks Club could have attempted to buy the mortgage back from us—we gave them notice of the proceedings—but they were not in attendance. We ended up buying back our own mortgage at the foreclosure sale. When we initially bought the mortgage from the bank, we had no right to the title for the property. The purchase of the note at the public auction fulfilled the steps required to complete our security interest, and gave us the title to the property that was held as collateral for the mortgage.

Once we gained possession of the title to the property, we again contacted the Elks to give them the option of honoring our contract. We didn't have to do this, since the property was already ours. But we wanted to try, one last time, to close the deal with them under amicable conditions to prevent any future lawsuits. The attorneys for the Elks Club would not consider our offer. We contacted Unity Church again, and let them know that everything was in place to close in February.

The closing with Unity Church went off without any problems. Our contract price remained the same: $950,000. Instead of making $400,000 profit on the deal, we cleared $725,000. Joe's warning of future litigation proved very prescient. In March, we received notice that we were being sued by the Elks Club. They contended that we did not properly conduct the auction for the sale of the mortgage in compliance with the rules set forth in the Uniform Commercial Code. In the lawsuit, they were seeking damages based on the profit from our sale of the property to Unity Church for $950,000.

It instantly became clear why the Elks Club refused to negotiate with us when we thought it was in their best interests: they were holding out for more money. That was why they would never sell the property to us at the original contract price of $550,000. My partner, Howard, and I each spent $100,000 over the course of the next 10 years battling the Elks Club in court. Eventually, the court ruled in our favor with prejudice, preventing the Elks from ever contesting the issue again. I was pleased to finally put the matter behind me, and glad that I was able to finance my defense using the extra proceeds from the deal.

When the Elks Club filed Chapter 7 bankruptcy, we were very impressed by their maneuver to legally rescind our contract and cut us out of the deal. Our move on the other hand—to purchase the mortgage and foreclose on the property—was even more than impressive. It was genius.

Joe Palmisano is no longer my attorney. As my company grew, our needs exceeded the capability of his small practice. I cherished those early years with Joe. Still to this day, when I am not in the room, Joe will take credit for the idea of purchasing the Elks Club mortgage as a way to get back into that deal. Joe may not know it, but I do: the credit really goes to Sam Zell. Had I never read about his purchase of the mortgage for the office tower in Salt Lake City, I would have never suggested the idea to Joe.

Early in my career, I learned the value of reading. Coming across the article on Sam Zell helped me salvage a deal that I thought was lost. I have found that, over the course of my career, some of the best lessons I have learned have come from other people's experiences.

Summary

Don't Be Greedy

All of the litigation could have been prevented had I never tried to flip the property before I had safely closed on the deal with the Elks Club. Agreeing to sell the property to Unity Church complicated the transaction and inadvertently introduced unnecessary parties into the original purchase. Unity Church should have never been in a position to jeopardize the deal. Keeping the details of a transaction confidential, only revealing them to a broker, banker, or partners, is critical to success.

Read for Keeps

Once the Elks Club used bankruptcy to get away from honoring our contract, I thought the deal was over. Discovering the means of buying the mortgage by reading the article about Sam Zell was priceless. The knowledge I gained allowed me to reinsert myself into the deal. This was one of my first experiences where my reading had paid dividends. It's a practice I have continued throughout my career and has repeatedly proven financially beneficial. Many people try to impress with their ability to read vast quantities of books and information. The true value of reading is realized when you uncover ideas and wisdom that can be implemented to solve problems in your own life's journey. Read to harness wisdom. Read for keeps.

Cash Is King

There is no substitute for having cash available when it is needed. This deal could have never been completed without the necessary cash to buy the back taxes and the mortgage. I knew I couldn't do it alone. I was able to obtain the cash that was needed from my father. The lesson I learned here was that I had to have money set aside, or equity partners ready, so that in the future when opportunity strikes, we are in a position to react immediately.

Avoid Litigation

We tried on multiple occasions to settle with the Elks Club in a friendly manner. My attorney, Joe Palmisano, advised me to avoid litigations at all costs. This advice came from a man who made his living as an attorney. We spent 10 years in litigation as a result of this deal, and the experience was draining. I would submit that, in most cases, a bad settlement is better than a good lawsuit.

Chapter 5

Failure in the Suburbs

Kenosha, Wisconsin & Merrillville, Indiana: 1991–1993

During the 1990 recession, I had stopped development in the Chicago urban market. I was literally going crazy. I had been working on different development projects practically non-stop for the previous 7 years. Everything came to a halt in 1990. I spent most of the year looking for new opportunities. No matter how hard I tried, I could not make anything happen. Toward the end of the year, I started to hear about developers having success with entry-level single-family homes in the Chicago suburbs. I had no experience in suburban development, but I figured I could at least look into it to see if there were opportunities I could explore.

I began by doing market research on entry-level suburban sites. Immediately, I was drawn to Kenosha, Wisconsin, a town located north of Chicago, just off of Interstate 94. Developments were starting to spring up in northern Lake County, Illinois, which was just south of Kenosha. Homes in this area were attractive to people who worked in the north I-94 corridor because it made for an easy commute. I was seriously considering my options. I had found a 60-acre parcel, on the south side of Kenosha, which was cheap by Chicago standards. Based on my research, I determined that housing could be sold in the $129,000 to $199,000 price range. These homes would be at affordable price points for the income levels of people migrating to the area. I did not know the suburbs like I knew the city, so I paid to have an independent market research study completed on the property before I moved forward with a project in the area.

The results of the study concluded that the Kenosha market would support a project like the one I had in mind. In late 1991, I created a partnership called Cumberland Homes, Ltd. for the new development and went ahead with the purchase of the 60-acre parcel. Another developer was already in the area. Their development was much larger, with a broader product line. I worked with a marketing consultant to design a product that was more upscale, at a slightly higher price point. Our development was called River Crossing.

Doing a residential development in the suburbs was different from an urban development. The entire infrastructure is already in place in the city. In the suburbs, we had to start with raw land and had to install all of the infrastructure components. There were no existing streets, sidewalks, sewers, or utilities; everything had to be built. The development was configured for 150 homes. The plan was to build the development in two phases, allowing us to start closing on the completed homes before starting on the second phase.

In early 1992, we built a model home and set up our sales center. Sales began coming in at a reasonable rate of five homes per month. We started the first phase of construction that spring. The excavation crew was the first to go in to start preparing the site for construction. About a week into the excavation, however, the project came to an abrupt halt when one of the excavators uncovered what he thought was wetlands. It was against the law to destroy wetlands, and none of the machine operators wanted to be held liable for destroying any wetlands. The area in question was about 10,000 square feet. No further excavation could be completed until the issue was resolved and the status of the land was verified.

I hired a Chicago environmental attorney, Janine Brown, to evaluate the situation and render her professional opinion. Ms. Brown slogged through the mud at the development site and personally inspected the land in question. She determined that the land was intermittent wetlands caused by farming. There was no need for us to take any measures to preserve this land. She provided me with a letter that stated her findings and would protect anyone working on our project from criminal prosecution. We had permission to continue with the excavation, but the state could still hold us civilly liable if they did not agree with Ms. Brown's findings. We wasted no more time, and moved forward with the excavation. The issue with the wetlands was never raised again.

After the short delay, development on infrastructure moved along smoothly. Once enough infrastructure was in place, we started to build the homes that were pre-sold. Each home took approximately 100 to 120 days to be completed. As the homes were finished, we closed on them as soon as possible. Generally, most of the buyers had made arrangements with their lenders to include an estimated amount in their monthly payment to be placed in escrow for their property taxes. We soon found out that the amount homeowners were allocating for their property taxes was only half of what was required. Somewhere, we had made a mistake. Property taxes on the homes in our development were double what we had estimated them to be. The impact of this revelation was still unknown.

River Crossing: 150 single-family homes in Kenosha, Wisconsin, on County H north of Highway 50.

The project in Kenosha had started off well and was initially showing signs of success. I wanted to find another area where I could duplicate that success. My father and his friend, Bud Fennema, owned a large 80-acre parcel of property in Merrillville, Indiana, near Interstate 65 and U.S. Route 30. They both invested in real estate as a side business, and supported the idea of a residential development on their property. I studied the demographics of the area, and determined that the household incomes were similar to those of Kenosha, Wisconsin. The area had not seen as much new construction in the previous 10 years as many other Chicago suburbs. I did not think the area was attractive for Chicago residents moving to the suburbs, but I believed the local market would support a more sophisticated, entry-level home than what was being built there.

The typical entry-level home in Merrillville was a 1,000-square-foot ranch with three bedrooms and no basement. I wanted to offer something better. I purchased the 80-acre parcel on contract from my father and Bud. The property was configured for 203 lots. I agreed to pay $1,000 up front for every lot and $4,000 after the closing of each home. The project was called The Preserves. I had four model homes built, ranging in size from 1,600 square feet to 2,400 square feet. The homes in the development would be priced from $129,900 to $199,900. For the next 60 days, we thought we'd hit a home run. Hundreds of potential buyers visited our sales center and toured the model homes. Our sales staff was frantic because they had never experienced traffic like this. They assured me sales would be spectacular.

Despite the traffic, we were only selling one to two homes per month. We needed to average four to five homes per month to be profitable. After 90 days, traffic started to slow down. Our visitors were more serious buyers, but we were still only averaging two homes per month.

The homes we were building in The Preserves were beautiful homes. They came with a view of a 20-acre wetland preserve. The price point for the homes was a little higher than other developments, but I thought buyers would be willing to pay more for a better product in this market. I soon found out that I was wrong. Even though the income levels were similar to other suburban Chicago entry-level markets, the typical homeowner in Merrillville was happy living more modestly. Instead of spending more on housing, they were likely to spend their disposable income on boats, jet skis, and recreational vehicles.

Back in Kenosha, the first phase of the development sold at a price point that was profitable for us. However, once buyers became aware of the higher property taxes in Kenosha County, sales slowed drastically. When the bill for the property taxes was factored into the cost of ownership, it was not worth it to move the few miles north to Kenosha from northern Illinois. Had the inverse been true, we would have been able to attract more buyers. We were competing directly with developments in Lake County, Illinois. Property taxes in Lake County, Illinois, were lower than in Kenosha, Wisconsin. We were forced to lower our prices to sell the final homes. I wanted to abandon the project, but we had to complete it in order to salvage some of the investment that was made in the infrastructure of the development. It was the only way I could pay off the bank loan for the project. The final seventy homes in River Crossing were each sold at a loss.

I was able to pay off the bank loan, but was unable to pay back our investors' equity. All of the equity was lost. I had to explain to our investors that I had failed. The loss of the investors' equity was evidence of the fact that I did not understand the risks of suburban development. It was one of the hardest moments in my life. All of my ventures from 1979 to 1991 had been successful. At 38 years old, I did not think it was possible for me to fail.

* * * * *

With the Kenosha project behind me, all I kept thinking about was getting back to the city. I was out of my element in the suburbs. In Bucktown, an area west of downtown Chicago, the urban market looked like it was gathering momentum. My friend and mentor, Bob Markey, had identified Bucktown in the late 1980s as the next area that was going to take off. I already owned a few properties there, but I started to acquire more in 1993 and 1994. I could lease these properties for a while, and wait for property values to increase. I was pleased to finally make some good business moves in the midst of all the failure I was experiencing.

The sales in Merrillville never took off. After just one year, we had only sold thirty-five homes. There were thirty vacant lots that were ready for construction in phase one of the development. No new buyers were coming forward, so we decided to cut our losses and shut down the project. There was no point in prolonging the inevitable. My father and Bud Fennema agreed to take back the remaining unimproved land. They understood the complications I had faced with the project. All $750,000 of the investor equity was lost. I contacted each investor individually, and explained what went wrong. The only thing left to do was negotiate a settlement with my lender, Bank One.

Originally the loan was with NBD, but at some point during the year, they were acquired by Bank One, which worked to my advantage. Bank One was more willing to negotiate with me in an effort to clean up their books. The outstanding balance on the loan was $1.5 million, and I had given my personal guarantee. The loan officer for Bank One proposed that the remaining thirty vacant lots within the subdivision be sold at a reduced price. The proceeds from the sale would be applied to the balance on the loan. The lots needed to be sold for at least $10,000. If the bank could not get this price, they informed me they would pursue me personally to further settle the debt.

I cooperated fully with the bank and turned over the titles

to the remaining lots. They were able to sell all thirty to one buyer at a price that was never disclosed to me. They chose not to hold me personally liable for the remaining balance, but the process did not happen overnight. Instead, the thought that the bank could seize my personal assets in an attempt to fulfill the debt obligation haunted me for about a year. When it was finally over, I felt a great weight lifted from my shoulders. I was ready to return to what I knew best: urban real estate development.

Reflecting on my failure in the suburbs made obvious the fact that I did not fully understand real estate development in the suburban markets where I was working. In Kenosha, I didn't research the local real estate taxes well enough to know how they would affect my buyers. Our developments were also smaller than the typical suburban developments. Larger builders were buying materials and services in far greater quantities then we were, and could receive them at a discount, giving them a competitive advantage over us in the same market, competing for the same buyer.

In the city, every project I developed was unique and different. It was not possible for builders in the city to obtain the competitive advantage of economy of scale like they could in the suburbs. The volume discount that a suburban developer might receive when doing a 1,000-home development could not be duplicated in the city. I was good at buying property at low prices and adding value through improvements. I recognized my ability to find and add value in the Chicago inner-city real estate market as a special skill that I possessed. I should have never strayed from my specialty.

While I was struggling with the failure of my projects in the suburbs, I would often go to the Barrington Club in South Barrington, Illinois, to exercise. I had been a member of the club for over 5 years. One day after working out, I ran into Bob Galvin, son of the founder of Motorola. From time to time, I would sit down with Bob for a cup of coffee before heading to work. I told Bob about my development projects in the suburbs and how this was my first real experience with failure in my career. Bob listened closely to what I was saying; he paused for a moment, and then asked if I had time for a story about his father.

Bob's father was an electronics genius who started Motorola with the two-way walkie-talkie during World War II. Bob said that after he graduated from Harvard, he went to work at Motorola for his father. One day, he went to his father to discuss his future. His father told him that he would probably never be as successful as him in his lifetime. Bob was shocked by this comment and asked his father why he thought that way. His father's reply was that, given the success of Motorola, Bob probably would never experience failure in his life.

In the early years of Motorola, the company almost went bankrupt. Bob Galvin learned from his father that failure, although painful, was the most important learning tool he had experienced in his life. Bob told me that I should embrace my failure because it was the best opportunity to learn lessons that most people will never have the chance to learn. Failure can ruin someone, but it can also strengthen a person's future business decisions. The willingness to persevere and learn from past mistakes was crucial for professional development.

I always had a lot of respect for Bob Galvin. He was a low-key, thoughtful businessman. He drove to the Barrington Club in a 10-year-old station wagon. His wisdom carried Motorola on for many decades, and his respect for failure helped him become highly successful in his life. The advice I received from Bob Galvin that day has stayed with me over the years. Anyone who knows me well can probably quote the story. I have told it many times and to many people. I make it a habit of letting people know that failure is a tool that can be used in achieving success in any part of their lives.

* * * * *

It was very difficult meeting with my investors and telling them I had lost their money. All of my investors were qualified investors, so at least it made things a little easier. Qualified investors meet specific requirements with regard to net worth and liquidity. Usually, they are savvier when it comes to investment decisions. They understand the risks associated with the investment, and that with any investment, there are no guarantees. Past performance is not a guarantee of future results. Qualified investors can afford to take the risks where an unqualified investor cannot. The loss of a $100,000 investment, while painful, will not financially ruin a qualified investor.

One of my investors in the River Crossing development in Kenosha, Wisconsin, was Bart Richards. Bart owned Arens Controls, a company that made control mechanisms for the aviation industry. In addition to being an investor of mine, I owed Bart $100,000 that he had loaned to me to buy an option on another parcel of land. Shortly after we started the River Crossing development, I thought that we should get a contract with the farmer that owned the adjacent parcel of land to give us the option to buy it at a later date. I was convinced that once our project was a success, the prices of vacant land in the area would shoot up. I wanted to lock in the deal at the current market prices.

The farmer agreed to sell us the option to buy the land for $100,000, which would be applied to the purchase price of $600,000, if we exercised the option within 3 years. I would lose the money if I failed to exercise the option within the allotted time period. The option was never exercised, and the $100,000 was gone. Bart knew that the project had been experiencing problems. I did not try to hide anything from him, or from any of my other investors; I kept him informed throughout the project. When it was over, he asked me to meet with him and his brother at his office in Evanston, Illinois.

One of the worst parts about losing Bart's money was that I was sure he would never invest with me again. River Crossing was the first project of mine in which he had invested. I figured the purpose of the meeting was to agree on some type of settlement for the loan. When I arrived at Bart's office, he was seated at his desk. I sat in the chair across from him on the other side. Directly in front of him was the promissory note that I had signed for the loan. His brother was in the office with us, standing off to the side of me. Some of the investments Bart made were in conjunction with his brother. He asked me to explain what happened with the River Crossing development again, so that his brother could hear the details straight from me.

I went over the entire story of how I had failed in Kenosha. I apologized repeatedly for losing their investment. When I finished, Bart looked up from his desk and said, "In regards to the $100,000 investment in River Crossing, I'm a big boy. I believed in the project just like you. I lost money, and I accept the loss." He paused for a moment and then continued, "Regarding the $100,000 note that you owe me, I suppose I could go after your house or other assets, but I decided I don't want to do that." He then lifted up the note in front of him and tore it in half and said, "Get out there, and find us some new deals to make money on!"

I was not expecting that meeting to turn out that way. When I left Bart's office, I vowed to myself that I would make it up to him. That money may have been lost, but he had made an investment in me that day. His confidence in me buoyed my self-esteem. I had never had anyone show so much faith in my ability to make them money, especially after losing over $1.5 million of investor equity in 3 years.

In 1993, I had a problem brewing at 2000 North Racine Avenue. This was our final historic rehab that we had converted into a shared office building. From 1990 to 1993, office rents both in Chicago and nationwide began to deteriorate. We had leased the entire building for $18 per square foot in 1987 on triple net leases. With a triple net lease, the owner of the building is only responsible for maintaining the exterior components of the property such as the structure, roof, and parking lot. The tenant is responsible for all other expenses. The $18-per-square-foot triple net lease was equivalent to a $22-per-square-foot gross lease. By 1993, we could only get $14 per square foot gross on the same space.

The loss of $8 per square foot reduced our income by $320,000 on the 40,000-square-foot building. The excess cash flow the building once generated had evaporated. There was not enough money to pay the mortgage, real estate taxes, and other expenses. We were forced to rob Peter to pay Paul for as long as we could, in an effort to survive until the market recovered. Eventually, we stopped making the mortgage payment and defaulted on the loan. We couldn't afford to continue to make the payments.

We had purchased the building for $500,000 and spent $2.7 million on the rehab. The investor equity amounted to $750,000, and our loan with Bank One was for $2.5 million. Defaulting on the loan would cause us to lose all of the investor equity. The investors had received good returns on their equity for the first 3 years the building was profitable. They also received their equity back in the form of an investment tax credit in the first year, but their initial investments were now gone.

It took 4 months for the bank to take control of the building. During that time, I continued to collect the rents. I accumulated over $100,000 in my checking account. I had given the bank my personal guarantee to further secure the loan when we initially obtained it. They agreed to release me from liability on the debt for a payment of $100,000. Luckily, I had the money on hand and was able to settle with the bank. At my last meeting with the officials from Bank One, I flippantly asked if I could buy the building back. The loan officer looked shocked, but he said that I could buy it back. I would have to pay cash, and they definitely would not finance me. Their appraiser would determine the value.

In 1987 when the property was originally financed, it was appraised at $3.5 million. The appraisal from the bank came back at $1.1 million, less than a third of the original appraised value. I loved this building, and I knew what it was worth. If the bank was willing to take $1.1 million for this building, it would be a fantastic deal for me, even if I was not emotionally attached to the property. I had to find a way to get it back. I contacted the bank and let them know that I wanted to buy the building. They kindly reminded me that I had to pay cash. I was given 2 days to find the money.

My first stop was to see Bart Richards. It had only been a few months since our last meeting. The last thing Bart had said to me was to find him some deals to make him some money. Well, I had found one. I laid out the deal for him, and he agreed to put up $200,000 for a 50% stake in the building. He did not even hesitate. He could see this deal was solid.

The next stop was at Midtown Bank. I had an old friend named Dave Grzenia, who was a banker there. I showed Dave the numbers on the deal and told him I had an investor who was putting up $200,000. Dave thought more like a businessman than a banker. I knew that if anyone could get this loan for $900,000 through a loan committee at a bank, it would be Dave.

Midtown Bank was closely held by a prominent business family in Chicago. They had a very open mind about looking at unique deals. Most banks would not be willing to finance a defaulted deal from another bank, especially when the buyer was the person who defaulted with the previous bank. The situation was not pretty. I needed Midtown Bank to focus on the extreme value of the asset and not on the borrower's past record of not paying the mortgage on time.

I convinced Bank One to give me a little more time to put the money together. Within a week, Dave called and was pleased to inform me that I got the loan. One of the members of the loan committee actually gave him a hard time for not finding deals like this for the bank to buy. They recognized the value in the building and overlooked my recent credit history. With the $900,000 from Midtown Bank and the $200,000 from Bart Richards, I closed on 2000 North Racine Avenue for the second time.

I refinanced the building a few years later and was able to return Bart's $200,000 investment. We held the building from 1994 to 2003. It generated steady cash flows the entire time. Bart received 50% of the net income for those 10 years and half the profit from the sale of the building in 2003. The building sold for $3.2 million. We each cleared around $1 million from the sale. It is safe to say that Bart was very pleased with the results from this deal.

Bart has invested in many projects of mine since his first investment with me in River Crossing in Kenosha. When I think I have a deal that is a winner, Bart is one of the first investors I contact. He has always believed in me, and I can never thank him enough for that. Still to this day, he has money invested with me.

Summary

Know Your Market

It is good to order appraisals or market reports to fine-tune your analysis about a specific market. Solely relying on those reports to make decisions, as I did, however, increases a development's risk. The suburbs were a black hole to me. I should have personally spent more time studying each location before beginning any projects. I knew exactly how Cook County set real estate taxes in Chicago. By not taking the time to understand Kenosha County and how they assessed real estate taxes, our development became exposed to a risk for which we had not sufficiently planned. When the homeowners received their tax bills, which were double our expectations, it became difficult to continue to sell homes at our price points. Had I taken the time to fully understand the market, I could have prevented the entire situation; having all of the information available to me in the beginning, I may have decided against the project.

Know Your Buyer

The Preserves in Merrillville presented another situation for which I was unprepared. Buyers in Chicago, and many other suburbs, prized homeownership and wanted the best home that they could afford. In Merrillville, the typical homebuyer had a different psyche. They valued lifestyle over having the best home. Their income was distributed amongst expenses that were uncommon for homeowners in the city; owning quality vehicles, RVs, and boats left little cash for housing expenditures. Merrillville homeowners seemed content with a small three-bedroom ranch, if it allowed them to maintain their lifestyles. Household income may have been the same in Merrillville as in Chicago, but I had no way of knowing the difference in the buyer's values. I was out of my element, and I did not invest the required time to sufficiently understand my prospective buyers.

Know Your Competition

In the city, I was usually ahead of the curve. In the suburbs, I was not ahead of anything. I was trying to jump on a trend that other developers, more experienced in suburban development, were already exploiting. I thought it was an opportunity that I could use to bridge the downtime in the urban market. What I discovered was that it was hard for me to compete with builders who specialized in suburban development. They had advantages of buying materials at lower costs and paying less for subcontractors due to long-term contracts and quantity discounts; these were opportunities that were not available to smaller scale developments like mine. I had to learn this lesson the hard way, and the results were costly. But the more expensive the lesson, the more likely it will be retained.

Good Relationships Are Priceless

Business is all about developing relationships. Despite my failure in the suburbs, something good resulted from it. The friendship that I have with Bart Richards has grown over the years. After I lost his money, he decided to give me another chance. He saw something in me that others did not. The confidence he had in me helped drive me to be successful. I will always be grateful to him for standing by my side.

Chapter 6

Experience and Capital Meet Bucktown

1993–1998

Bucktown is a one-square-mile area of Chicago about 2 miles northwest of downtown. In the 1800s, it was a small town previously known as Holstein. Back then, it was common practice in Holstein to own male goats, called bucks, and for residents to keep these bucks fenced in their yards on their property. The practice became so popular that people began to refer to Holstein as Bucktown. When Holstein was incorporated into the city of Chicago, the name Bucktown remained when referring to this neighborhood. In 1994, I was ready to risk everything I had on Bucktown; I was not going to miss this opportunity.

The memories of my difficulties in the suburbs were fading. I was definitely ready to put the entire experience behind me. In 1994, I met with Bob Markey, who had always been a source of quality advice in my life. I rode in the car with Bob as he drove around Bucktown, showing me the properties he had bought from 1990 to 1994. He also pointed out properties that he thought I should investigate. Bob encouraged me to focus my attention on Bucktown; he saw how Bucktown was evolving much like DePaul did in the 1980s. It again struck me that the city was what I knew best. Talking with Bob while we toured around Bucktown was the jumpstart I needed to get back into inner-city development. I knew that whatever I did, I wanted to be near the action. According to Bob, the action was going to be there, in Bucktown.

One of the properties Bob had suggested to me was a 25,000-square-foot parcel at 1800 North Hoyne Avenue. The parcel was owned by Aldi Foods and was contiguous with their store at 1801 North Milwaukee Avenue. They had used the vacant lot for years to drop clean fill and concrete, which was from their new store construction sites in the Chicago area. I had calculated that the property could be configured for seven single-family lots. There already were single-family homes and three-flats on two sides of the property. Still, the parcel would have to be rezoned from M1-1 industrial to R-4 residential, which I didn't consider an issue since my plan was in line with the existing homes in the immediate area.

I contacted Aldi headquarters in Batavia, Illinois, to see if they would consider selling the parcel. I offered to pay $100,000, and they agreed, having no other use for the property. As a condition of the sale, I was responsible for clearing the lot of all the debris that had been left behind. It was not a bad stipulation, especially at the price I paid for the property. I contracted to have the site cleared for $30,000, putting my cost basis for the seven lots at less than $20,000 per lot. The memory of seeing lots in DePaul purchased for $25,000, and resold, one year later, for $100,000, was playing over and over again in my mind. As my father's friend Bud Fennema would say, "A property that is bought right is half sold." That is exactly how I felt after acquiring this property.

Two aldermen had jurisdiction over separate parts of Bucktown. The area west of Milwaukee Avenue was in Alderman Billy Ocasio's ward. The remainder of Bucktown, south of Fullerton Avenue, east of Milwaukee Avenue and north of North Avenue, was in Alderman Terry Gabinski's ward. Since there was so much development occurring in Bucktown, an official community organization—The Bucktown Community Organization (BCO)—was formed by a group of area residents in Alderman Gabinski's ward. This organization was created to ensure the neighborhood interests were taken into consideration when planning new development projects.

I presented my plan for the seven single-family lots to the BCO. They commended me for bringing a single-family development to Bucktown. Most of the new development had been condos, which were not particularly attractive to families, and the BCO was trying to encourage families to move to the area. Their belief was that young families would give balance to the changing neighborhood. The R-4 zoning I was seeking would allow me to build three-flats, but I promised the BCO that I would only build single-family homes if my zoning was approved. My zoning request was approved by them. I then had to present my proposal to the alderman.

Alderman Gabinski would be responsible for getting my zoning petition placed on the next zoning committee meeting agenda. Once I had the support of the community through the BCO, it was just a formality to get the alderman's approval. I made an appointment to meet the alderman at his office. I had a portfolio of drawings and renderings prepared, to show him how the project would look.

In my numerous encounters with aldermen, I found that they were always late. They dealt with so many various neighborhood issues that every day was organized chaos, putting them almost always behind schedule.

I should not have been surprised; Alderman Gabinski was no different. He was running late when he finally greeted me and invited me into his office. He looked distracted as I presented my plan for the seven lots on North Hoyne Avenue. When I finished, he broke the news to me that a new community organization, West Bucktown Neighbors, had formed as a result of my zoning request, specifically to oppose my project. I could not believe what I was hearing. I explained to him how the "official" Bucktown Community Organization overwhelmingly approved of my project. He said his hands were tied, and that I had to make this new group happy before we could move forward with the zoning request.

I met once a month for 3 months with the West Bucktown Neighbors. After several meetings, it became clear that this group would not support any development at my site. They all lived near the site and were opposed to any change. Before the fourth meeting, I called Alderman Gabinski with an idea I was sure would make his life easier. I told him that I wanted him to inform the West Bucktown Neighbors that I was requesting that he formally reject my zoning request at the next zoning committee meeting. He was understandably confused. I explained that if he formally denied my zoning request, I would be able to file a lawsuit to sue for unrestricted R-4 zoning. Since the natural zoning of the neighborhood was residential, I was likely to win. Once I prevailed in court, I planned to build seven three-flats, instead of the seven single-family homes that I had originally promised.

The alderman felt my request was reasonable. He said he would pass on the message. I later learned from him that at his next meeting with the West Bucktown Neighbors, he first asked if they still objected to my development. They hadn't changed their minds. He informed them that he was going to honor my request to formally deny my zoning petition. This statement made no sense to them either. They could not understand why I would want the alderman to formally deny my request for zoning. That had been the primary goal of their organization from day one.

Alderman Gabinski then relayed to them my plan to sue the city to get the residential zoning. He outlined to them how the zoning I was requesting was harmonious with the neighborhood, and that I had a good chance of winning a lawsuit against the city. Then he dropped my well-planned bomb; he told them that I was no longer planning to build single-family homes on the site. After suing for unrestricted R-4, they learned that if successful, I planned to build seven three-flats instead. That news gained their attention. Under the original plan, I was restricting myself to building single-family homes. I knew they wanted the property to remain vacant, but I also knew they would much rather see seven single-family homes than seven three-flats. They asked the alderman to step out while they discussed the situation privately amongst themselves.

Human beings are funny creatures. In my experience, even when a development is economically good for them, some will protest against it. Many people are afraid of change. After about 10 minutes, the alderman was invited back into the room. When he stepped back into the meeting with the West Bucktown Neighbors, they had miraculously changed their minds. They approved my original proposal for R-4 residential zoning for the seven single-family lots. With their blessing, the alderman was able to proceed with the zoning request at the next zoning committee meeting.

I never understood the motivation behind the West Bucktown Neighbors to stop the development on my site. Change may be the most inevitable reality in our lives, and thankfully, I was able to convince them that my original plan was not that bad by showing them how my alternative course of action was incrementally worse. By approving my original request, they restricted me to single-family home sites, which, for them was the lesser of two evils. Of course, with the unrestricted R-4 zoning, the only thing that prevented me from building three-flats on those lots was my word. It is safe to say that if I went against my word and built those three-flats, I would have had a difficult time getting anything else zoned in the area for a long time. People in Chicago have long memories. They neither forgive nor forget very easily.

When I purchased this parcel, I knew that I was buying it cheap, and would have to pay taxes on the capital gains when I eventually sold it. Buying it at such a discount meant that when the market took off, most of the proceeds from the sale were going to be capital gains. I chose to do this deal alone and deviate from my usual methods of acquiring properties. I opted to purchase it through my retirement plan. This option was more complex, but it allowed me to defer the taxes on any capital gains until I retired or reached the age of 59 ½ and withdrew the funds. I was essentially giving up some of the control of the asset for the tax benefits. In the end, I held the lots until 1998, when I sold them to an area broker/developer for $1.1 million. I made him sign an agreement that he would only develop single-family homes on the seven lots.

In DePaul in the 1980s, I had only done a mediocre job of buying enough properties to create wealth. I was prepared to be more dominant in this new market. If Bucktown followed the same pattern, I wanted to be positioned to better take advantage of the rise in property values. On my own, I was purchasing as many houses and vacant lots as I could afford. I also partnered with an area real estate broker, Bill Senne, to acquire other Bucktown real estate. Having Bill as a partner gave me an inside track to identify the newest listings as soon as they became available.

Bill was a talented real estate broker who owned his own realty business, Property Consultants. Together we purchased over fifty different properties in Bucktown. We kept thirty-six properties in a portfolio that was managed by his company. The rest of the properties were flipped to a builder or developer, sometimes as fast as we could close on the deals. On many occasions, we had a contract to purchase a vacant lot or a home, and within a week, we would already have it resold. Sometimes, we would just sell our contract to buy a property to another buyer, and they would close on the purchase.

The market was hot. We were constantly moving in and out of properties. I did not press my luck again with back to back closings after my experience with the Elks Club in 1988. Instead, we would typically purchase a property for cash, close within days, and then resell the property to our new buyer. Ideally, we would have liked to have held the properties for at least a year and a day to avoid paying the higher short-term capital gains taxes. Many times it probably would have been in our best interests to hold the property because values were only rising. But the money was simply too good to refuse.

It was a great partnership with Bill Senne. We were able to acquire some of the best real estate in Bucktown. In the summer of 1995, Bill found a vacant, 200,000-square-foot, three-story loft building at 2300 West Wabansia Avenue that was the former site of the Kling Brothers Clothing manufacturing facility. The building had a unique feature: there was a clock tower built into the facade. It was a very distinctive building that I thought would be perfect to convert into loft condominiums. The current owner had been leasing the space to various tenants and saw the opportunity to cash in on the booming real estate market. The building was listed for $2.4 million. I wanted to buy this property, but I needed help raising equity; Bill and I could not finance this project alone.

2300 W. Wabansia Avenue: Clocktower Lofts – 113 unit building developed in 1996 in the Bucktown neighborhood.

Naturally, I turned to my accountant, Bob Finnigan, for help. Bob had been my partner in the 1980s, while doing historic rehabs and for-sale development. He did not partner with me on the projects in the suburbs, which probably played to my benefit, because he might not have taken a chance on this new project. I brought a copy of my contract to purchase 2300 West Wabansia Avenue to his office. I explained my plan to convert the property into loft condominiums. Bob agreed to begin raising equity for us. Bill Senne and I both put up equity and together with Bob and our investors, we purchased the building and began the project. Over time, Clocktower Lofts evolved as the name for the development.

The property for Clocktower Lofts was in an industrial area, requiring us to get it rezoned before we could start construction there. Our property was on the portion of Wabansia Avenue that is west of Milwaukee Avenue, falling within the borders of Alderman Ocasio's ward.

Alderman Ocasio had just been elected as alderman in 1994. He took over the position from Luis Gutierrez, who had been elected U.S. Congressman for the fourth congressional district of Illinois. Congressman Gutierrez had served as alderman for 8 years before moving on to the U.S. House of Representatives. During Alderman Ocasio's early years in office, Congressman Gutierrez served as a mentor to him. Alderman Ocasio did not have any real experience in politics when he became alderman, and Congressman Gutierrez helped him find his way in the beginning.

Congressman Gutierrez would assist Alderman Ocasio with the requests for zoning in his ward. Sometimes, this would create a logistical problem for us since we were in Chicago, and Congressman Gutierrez was in Washington, D.C. This problem was easily remedied by our zoning attorney, Bill Singer, of Kirkland & Ellis. Singer frequently flew to Washington, D.C., for other business and would meet with Congressman Gutierrez to get preapproval for our zoning requests. The congressman would then discuss the proposals with Ocasio. If they both approved of the project, then we had the green light to set up a meeting to present the project to the community.

I never met Billy Ocasio or Luis Gutierrez until 1997, even though we first got started in Bucktown a few years earlier. The attorneys handled all the interactions with politicians related to our zoning petitions, giving me more time to focus on real estate development. The meetings with the community were usually facilitated by one of the alderman's staff members. Clocktower Lofts was my first major project in Bucktown. There was no opposition to our development from the community. Everyone seemed to be on board with the transformation that was going on in Bucktown. Our proposal made it through the zoning committee and the city council with no resistance.

Clocktower Lofts was one of the best development projects of my career. Construction went smoothly, there were no cost overruns, and buyers loved the finished product. Bill Senne's company, Property Consultants, handled all of the marketing and sales for the project. There were a total of 113 units, and they sold in 120 days. In real estate development, that is fast. We knew we had a hot product, and could have raised our price as soon as we saw how fast they were selling, but I didn't want to get greedy. I was happy to be selling at a profit after my troubling experience in the suburbs.

The conventional wisdom for architects designing apartments or condominiums was that a one-bedroom unit should be at least 700 to 800 square feet, and a two-bedroom unit should be at least 1,100 to 1,200 square feet. They were designing a product to specifications they thought the buyer would require. I, on the other hand, wanted to have a product designed to specifications I thought the buyer could afford. I had instructed our architects, when designing Clocktower Lofts, to make one-bedroom units between 550 to 650 square feet and two-bedroom units between 900 to 1,050 square feet. We found out quickly that buyers were willing to accept smaller living spaces, at affordable prices, in order to live in this vibrant neighborhood.

At Clocktower Lofts, the average one-bedroom loft sold for $110,000, and the average two-bedroom loft sold for $150,000. Our largest units sold for $199,000. At these prices, we outsold every competing development in the area. I attribute our success to our design and pricing. Buyers recognized the added value they instantly received upon closing. Once all of the units were sold, there were a few buyers who flipped their units for a 10% to 20% profit. Today, a home in Clocktower Lofts is even more coveted, because Bucktown is one of the most desired places to live in Chicago. Lofts in the development still sell for more than double the price at which they were originally sold in 1996.

I always tried to have multiple irons in the fire. While construction was taking place at Clocktower Lofts, I continued to buy and sell properties through my partnership with Bill Senne. Around this same time, I was also continuing to buy homes on my own. I discovered that a lot of property owners were not using a broker to list their properties, but instead, they were listing their properties as for sale by owner in the *Chicago Tribune*. The new listings would show up every Saturday in the classified section of the paper. Every Saturday, I would search the paper for listings in and around Bucktown. The listings were usually priced so cheap that by the time I responded to the ad, the property was already sold. My wife, Marla, discovered that the same ads that appeared in Saturday's paper were available online the Tuesday before publication. This was our chance to get a leg up on the competition.

One rainy Tuesday evening, as I was driving home, Marla called with an address for a listing in Bucktown. The ad for the property had just appeared on the *Chicago Tribune*'s website that day. I was going in the opposite direction, so I turned the car around and headed straight for the address. I always kept copies of my standard contract in the car, in case I came across properties I wanted to buy.

The listing turned out not to be in Bucktown, but about a block away, right on the edge of Wicker Park in the 1500 block of North Elk Grove Avenue. This was a great area—the revitalization progress that was being made in Bucktown was bleeding over into Wicker Park. The home was listed for $69,000.

On the way to the property, I called the homeowner and asked if I could come by to see the house. She was surprised to get such a quick response from her ad. She agreed to allow me to see the house.

The homeowner wanted to sell the home so she could move to the suburbs in northern Indiana. I offered to pay the full asking price. The value of the purchase to me was in the lot; the existing structure would have to be demolished.

I knew the vacant lot alone was worth more than her asking price. She agreed to sell the property to me, and we signed a purchase agreement in her living room that evening. At the closing, she told me she had received over twenty inquiries about the house. She informed them that it was already sold, and some people even offered to pay more than her asking price. She chose to honor our contract.

I held on to the house for about a year before selling it to a builder for $150,000. He demolished the house and built a three-flat in its place. The beautiful thing about the small properties we were buying and selling was that they did not need to be rezoned. A builder could demolish the existing structure and rebuild within the existing zoning. Many of the properties were zoned R-4 residential, which allowed up to three separate units on one lot. Homeowners eventually discovered that they could get more money by listing their homes through a broker. It is a broker's job to understand the market and help the seller price their property accordingly. I was able to buy a handful of homes through the "For Sale by

Owner" listings in the paper. After a while, these listings started to dry up. I still bought plenty of properties that were listed through a broker, but these deals were never as good. I told everyone I knew to buy property in Bucktown. Everyone who listened, including my sister and father, did well with their investments. I wish I still had some of the properties I had sold in Bucktown over 15 years ago. Even with the real estate market crash and recession, at the prices I paid in the 1990s, the properties I owned there would still be solid investments.

Everything seemed to happen all at the same time in Bucktown. Development was moving so fast that it was hard for me to keep up. My advantage was my partnership with Bill Senne. He and his staff managed all of the properties we owned together, and handled all of the sales and marketing for my development projects in Bucktown. On top of all of that, Bill would bring me some of the best deals in the area. If we could do a deal by ourselves, we would. If not, we would call in Bob Finnigan to raise equity. In the summer of 1996, Bill found a site on West Bloomingdale Avenue that was a fantastic deal. He personally signed a contract to buy it and then brought it to me to figure out how we would pay for it.

The property was the former site of the A&B Safe Company in the 2300 block of West Bloomingdale Street. The site consisted of eighteen individual lots that at one time had been zoned residential. Bill had a contract to buy the lots for $900,000. I knew it would have to be rezoned, but that was just a technicality. Between the two of us, we did not have the cash to finance the deal. This was much bigger than the lots and single-family homes we had been purchasing through our partnership. I thought that we could get it done without outside investors, because the property was worth more than the $900,000 we were paying. It would be worth at least double once it was rezoned as residential. I was sure that I could find a bank to loan us the money.

I presented the deal to Dave Grzenia at Midtown Bank. Dave had financed my first deal in DePaul back in 1983 at Ravenswood Bank. I had developed a good relationship with both him and the bank over the course of our business transactions. I was confident they would give me the loan based on my credit history and how solid this deal was. They agreed to finance 100% of the purchase price. Bill and I were 50-50 partners, and neither of us had to put up a dime.

2300 W. Bloomingdale Avenue: Zoned in 1997 and resold to two other companies who built townhomes and condominiums.

Shortly thereafter, we discovered a 40,000-square-foot industrial building at 1751 N. Western Avenue, right next to the eighteen lots we had just purchased. The building was vacant. It had previously been an electrical component maker that had been gone for years. Construction was still ongoing at Clocktower Lofts, but I needed to find another site for our next development. Our formula worked well at Clocktower Lofts, and I knew we could use the same basic design concepts and price points with this building, just on a smaller scale. This site was not very large, but it would work for thirty to thirty-five lofts. We secured a contract to buy the property for $600,000. Bob Finnigan raised the equity for the purchase and construction of the development.

I was focusing my attention on a smaller subsection of Bucktown, west of Milwaukee Avenue, that formed a triangle shaped area with Western Avenue and Wabansia Avenue. This was the only part of Bucktown that had larger buildings that could be converted into multi-unit loft buildings. I was more interested in buildings where I could put thirty or more units. That was where the money was in Bucktown development. Smaller development projects could still be profitable, but the larger projects scaled better. With a larger project, it was as easy to build thirty units as it was to build three. Our design and pricing at Clocktower Lofts was very popular with the buyers. I wanted to find multiple buildings where we could implement the same strategy. I found one such building on the north side of the 2300 block of West St. Paul Avenue.

The building was owned by a Santa Monica, California businessman named Meyer Luskin. I called Mr. Luskin directly, and offered him $900,000 for the building. I determined this was a fair offer considering the prices we had been paying for other properties in the area. The facility was a bakery goods recycling plant where old bakery goods were recycled into food products for animals. A few days after I had made my offer, Mr. Luskin called to inform me that he had another offer from a potential buyer for $1 million. He asked me if I wanted to increase my bid. I increased my bid to $1.1 million. We then went back and forth in a bidding war over the course of a week, in increments of $50,000 and $100,000, until I had made my last bid at $1.3 million. At this point, I was becoming concerned that I could not bid higher, and safely make a profit on the development of the site.

I wanted this property, but I did not want to pay more than $1.3 million to acquire it. I had to do something to put an end to the bidding war. I called Mr. Luskin and asked him what his plans were for the recycled bakery goods company that he was operating at the site. He said that the business was highly profitable, and he planned to buy an industrial site in the suburbs and build a new 40,000-square-foot building for his operation. I paused for a second on the phone, then suggested that I buy the land for him in the suburbs and stand in as its owner while the new facility was built. We would postpone the closing on the property in Bucktown until the new location was ready in the suburbs. Then, he could do a 1031 exchange, and transfer the proceeds from the sale of the old property toward the purchase of the new property tax-free.

2300 West St. Paul Avenue: 80 Condominiums. This included four 20-unit buildings. Zoned in 1997, and resold in 2000 to another company.

A 1031 exchange allows a property owner to roll the gain from the sale of an investment property over to the purchase of a new investment property, and avoid paying taxes on the gain. Mr. Luskin was not familiar with 1031 exchanges, but I definitely had his attention. He was interested in my proposal, but first he had to consult his attorney before making a decision. The next day, he called me back and said we had a deal. I was ecstatic that this idea was valuable enough to him to stop the bidding at $1.3 million.

We signed a contract and locked in my final bid as the selling price. I had his permission to move forward with a request for a change in the zoning on the property during this period, although I did not own the building, and while the new facility in the suburbs was built. I worked with representatives from Mr. Luskin's company to identify a location in the suburbs. They finally identified a site after many months of searching. I signed on as owner and construction began almost immediately. With the acquisition of this site, and the two other properties I purchased through partnerships that needed to be rezoned as residential, I contacted my zoning attorney, Bill Singer, to handle all the details. As soon as Clocktower Lofts was finished, I wanted to move on to the next project.

The three properties were all located in Alderman Ocasio's ward. Bill Singer facilitated the zoning proposals for the sites. Both Congressman Gutierrez and Alderman Ocasio supported our development projects. They saw it as an opportunity to bring much needed revitalization to an area that had become rundown and infested with crime. It was the right thing to do, but it was not in their own self-interest, a driving force that is so common in politics. The transplants that moved into these new housing developments in Bucktown during the 1990s were not what would be considered their ideal constituency. To put it another way, the white, middle-class residents who had moved into Bucktown did not normally vote for Alderman Ocasio or Congressman Gutierrez in later elections. Think for a moment how transformed our country would be if our politicians, at the national level, made decisions like these that are good for the common good of society, but not necessarily for the good of their careers. Unfortunately,

Washington does not work that way.

The zoning of these properties was approved by the city with no opposition. However, it would still be a while before the site at 2300 West St. Paul was ready for construction; the new facility in the suburbs was nowhere near completion. We were contemplating the development of the eighteen lots on Bloomingdale Avenue, but we still did not have a solid plan in place for that project. The easiest transition for us was to continue building loft condominiums at our site at 1751 N. Western Avenue, the former electrical component company.

One of the privileges of being a developer is that I get to select the name for our developments. These names will still be there long after I am gone from this world. I was very creative in the selection of the name for this project: Electric Co. Lofts. There was nothing extraordinary about this project. The most fulfilling aspect was in the application of our strategy and seeing it all come to fruition. We were not trying to recreate the wheel. We knew what was working for us, and we stuck with it. I wanted to stay with entry-level development, while many developers were attracted to the higher profit margins of more upscale development. There were more potential buyers in the entry-level market, and I did not want any problems selling the completed units.

The interior demolition of the building began in late 1996. We kept the exterior shell of the structure and added new windows and doors. Construction began in December 1996, and by May 1997 we had pre-sold all thirty-five units. The building was four stories. The bottom level was reserved for the lobby and parking, with the lofts on the top three levels. The building was very popular with young, single professionals and couples without children. It offered top-quality housing in one of Chicago's best neighborhoods.

Bucktown was becoming the place to live. Crime rates went down throughout the area as new development expanded. In the 1980s, on a trip down North Avenue between Damen Avenue and Ashland Avenue, one would encounter prostitutes on both sides of the street. Such experiences no longer existed in the late 1990s. These improvements contributed to Bucktown's rapid growth and the demand for real estate. The vacant lots that we owned on Bloomingdale Avenue were becoming very valuable. I was wrestling with the idea of flipping the lots to another developer. At the current market rates, I figured we could make more money by flipping them rather than developing single-family homes on the lots. We had enough projects going on at the time that I did not want us to overburden ourselves with a new-construction development. Our other developments had both been rehabs of existing structures, which were then converted into multi-unit loft buildings. The best solution was to sell the lots.

This was the property that Bill Senne and I had purchased together for $900,000, financed entirely by Midtown Bank. For over a year, we had been receiving offers to buy our land. Finally in the summer of 1997, we accepted an offer for $3.2 million. The developers planned to build eighty townhomes and condominiums on the site. The offer was too good for us to turn down. After the closing, Bill and I each walked away with over $1 million profit. With no equity of our own invested, our return was not even calculable. It was infinite.

The supply of available industrial buildings, in the subsection of Bucktown in which we were focusing, was diminishing. Next door to Clocktower Lofts was one of the last available properties in 1997. It was a vacant 40,000-square-foot building located at 2210 W. Wabansia Avenue. The building was the same size as Electric Co. Lofts, and I purchased it for $600,000, or $15 per square foot.

I recognized that I could be more profitable doing rehabs instead of new construction. In DePaul during the 1980s, our rehabs were very profitable because of the investment tax credit. The rehabs we were doing in Bucktown had a more aesthetic appeal than new construction, and with the market demand, we had a lot of success with our product.

The development was known as Pinnacle Lofts. The building we were rehabbing was a one of a kind, triangle-shaped structure that ran parallel to Winnebago Avenue. It made for a contemporary look, but a very radical design. The building had parking on the first level and ten lofts on each of the upper three levels. The configuration of the floors resulted in one unit with two exterior walls instead of one per floor. Not knowing what else to do, we installed balconies on both walls to maintain the symmetry of the exterior appearance. The odd-shaped lofts appealed to buyers willing to sacrifice living space for the luxury of these unique condos.

2210 W. Wabansia Avenue: Pinnacle Lofts, 30-unit loft building.

We did not encounter any difficulties selling the lofts. Bill Senne's company, Property Consultants, again handled all of the sales and marketing for the project. There was still great demand for affordable, residential housing in Bucktown. When we started Pinnacle Lofts, we did not know it would be our last project in the neighborhood. We were planning to develop the site that I was in the process of purchasing from Meyer Luskin at 2300 West St. Paul Avenue.

By early 1998, construction on the new facility for the recycled bakery goods factory was nearing completion. I was starting to become nervous that Meyer Luskin would withdraw from our deal. In the almost 2 years from the time I had signed the contract for $1.3 million, the property had greatly increased in value. All of the other buildings in the surrounding area had either been demolished or renovated, and this last building was becoming an eyesore to the neighborhood. They wanted something done with it. I had it rezoned as R-5 residential, which would allow one dwelling unit for every 400 square feet of land area, equivalent to a maximum of eighty units on the site. The community, including some of the very customers who had purchased lofts from me in surrounding buildings, started to think the development of eighty units at that site was too dense for the neighborhood.

I flew to California to meet face to face with Meyer Luskin. I did not tell him I was coming. I considered it a family vacation. I had never met him, and I wanted to ensure that there was nothing to prevent the closing on the building. We were only weeks away from the closing. My wife and son both accompanied me on the trip. We spent a week in Palm Springs, about an hour-and-a-half from Santa Monica. When I arrived in Palm Springs, I called Mr. Luskin, told him I was in the area, and asked if he would like to meet my wife and me for dinner. He was pleased to receive my call and graciously accepted my offer.

We lined up a babysitter for my son, then my wife and I drove to Santa Monica for the day. We arrived very early, so I dropped her off in an area shopping district and headed for Mr. Luskin's office. I wanted to stop in and see if he was available. He had some business he was finishing up, but he wrapped things up quickly and made time for me. I had originally pictured Mr. Luskin as a mid-level executive. Boy, was I wrong! It became evident, as I sat in his office watching his interactions with people, that he was a very powerful businessman. He assured me that everything was in place for our closing, and there were no problems on his end. What was seemingly a big deal to me, was hardly worthy of concern to him. I was worried for no reason. He wasn't concerned about the increasing value of the property. I could tell by the type of businessman he was, he would never withdraw from a contract.

When I returned from California, we closed on the property at 2300 West St. Paul Avenue. Word traveled quickly in Bucktown, and, within days, we had multiple offers to purchase the property. The opportunity to sell the property was starting to look better than trying to develop the site. Only Bob Finnigan and I had put up equity to purchase the building. If we wanted to develop the site, we would have had to take on investors. In addition, the development would not be our ideal project. The building had to be demolished, and everything had to be new construction. Our operation was more geared for doing rehabs. We had built a few townhome developments in the city and subdivisions in the suburbs from the ground up, but in recent years we had focused primarily on rehabbing.

The decision was made to sell the site to a developer who wanted to build four twenty-unit buildings. His design complied with the existing zoning. We signed a contract to sell the property for $4.2 million, $2.9 million over our acquisition price. Around the same time, the neighborhood had become vocal against the development of this site. My buyer was purchasing the land with the expectation that it would remain zoned R-5. I had to do everything in my power to deliver it to him as promised, or there would be no sale.

The biggest complaint the neighbors had with the site was that they believed the development of eighty dwelling units at the location was too dense. This argument was ridiculous. The majority of the immediate area, including the buildings which these protesters lived in, had the same R-5 zoning. What worried me the most was that Alderman Ocasio was listening to their concerns. I understood these were his voters and he had to kowtow to them, but this was the zoning that he had agreed to almost 2 years ago. We had invested a lot of time and resources getting the zoning in the first place. They wanted to restrict us to R-4 zoning, which would permit one dwelling unit for every 900 square feet and thereby cut the allowable units to forty-two.

If the zoning was changed, our buyer was out. The reality of the situation was that the site would support four twenty-unit buildings better than fourteen three-flats. The neighborhood did not realize how much more congruent the four larger buildings would be with the surrounding structures. Fourteen smaller buildings would have looked out of place on St. Paul Avenue. I had to get a handle on the situation before it got out of control. My best option was to call Congressman Gutierrez for help.

The first time I met Congressman Gutierrez was in 1997, at a fundraiser held at Jane's restaurant in Bucktown. I was a little uncomfortable because I did not know what to expect. My apprehension was put to rest the moment Congressman Gutierrez shook my hand. I immediately felt comfortable in his presence; he was very personable and easy to talk to. I could see why he had been so successful in politics; he was charismatic, and his voters adored him. He regularly received 80% to 90% of the votes in his district. I became good friends with Congressman Gutierrez and grew to look forward to our conversations, where we shared ideas and advice.

In 1998, the only real estate I still owned in Bucktown was the thirty-six properties that were in a partnership with Bill Senne. In 2000, I decided I wanted to sell my share of the portfolio, cash out of residential real estate and focus on the acquisition of industrial properties. I believed industrial real estate would provide greater cash flows, in the long run. We divided the thirty-six properties into two pools of eighteen, and Bill and I each selected a pool. I sold my share, but Bill kept his. As of 2011, Bill Senne still owned his eighteen properties from our partnership, and has since added many more to his portfolio. He owns some of the best real estate in Bucktown today.

Summary

Find a Mentor; Be a Mentor

Bob Markey was an important mentor to me in the city of Chicago. He helped me refocus my attention on Bucktown, and move away from my failure in the suburbs. Throughout my career, he has always been a great source of advice and direction for me. I attribute much of my success to his guidance and instruction. Having a good mentor is essential to success. There isn't anyone better to learn from, than someone who has already done it. I was fortunate to meet Bob early in my career. I cannot imagine the mistakes I might have made without his counsel. Also, never pass up an opportunity to mentor others.

Get Involved in the Community

A local developer is likely to have more success, in their own community, than an outsider. That is why it is so important that a developer gets involved in the community early in the process. Neighborhood groups can be obstacles to obtaining zoning within a community. Having a good reputation—not only as a builder, but also as a member of the community—is important. The promise of quality development many times is not enough. Some communities have a no-growth position toward any development. It is a difficult position to go up against. The best approach is to get involved in the community, in any way possible, and show a vested interest. This, along with good design and top-quality construction, will help a developer gain community support.

Hire the Best Experts

As our development projects began to increase in size, I realized how important it was to hire the best experts in their respective fields for my team. Zoning was a major issue in Bucktown. Hiring Bill Singer as my zoning attorney was the right decision. He was a man who could get the job done. His understanding of the neighborhood politics allowed me to focus on the business side of our projects, while he handled the zoning. Having good people on my team gave me the peace of mind that the job would be done properly.

Let Your Best Instincts Prevail

A serious problem we faced in real estate development was that buyers were being priced out of the market. Architects were dictating the design specifications of condominium units based on what they believed the buyer in the target market wanted. What resulted was a product that some buyers could not afford. My solution to the problem was to determine how much a buyer could afford, and work back from there to set the design specifications. Our units were a little smaller than what had been standard in the marketplace, but the response from our buyers was overwhelmingly positive. We had no difficulty selling the completed units. Solving a problem can give a business an advantage over the competition, at least until the competition discovers that same strategy.

Exploit Market Inefficiencies

My wife discovered that "For Sale by Owner" ads appeared online 4 days before the print versions. This discovery gave us an advantage. We were able to receive the information and get a property under contract before many people even knew it was for sale. Identifying the inefficiency of a process, and determining what it takes to make the process more efficient, is key in finding an advantage in business.

There Is No Substitute for Hard Work

Unlike the real estate gurus who make outrageous promises about how someone can get rich quick on "no money down" deals, I am here to say that there is no substitute for hard work and real equity. In my career, I have only obtained 100% financing on one deal. Of the numerous properties I have purchased in over the past 30 years, it has happened only one time, when I purchased the former A&B Safe Company. I got lucky that one time. All of the other deals required plenty of hard work, equity, and perseverance, which paid off in the end.

Chapter 7

A Design Decision Creates a Lifetime of Profit

Ameritech: 1998–2000

In the fall of 1997, we were still working on Pinnacle Lofts, our last project in Bucktown. Since I knew it would be our final project there, I wanted to find a part of town where my competitors were not developing. The Loop caught my eye. There had been no significant residential development in the Loop, Chicago's central office district, since the late 1970s. The last development had involved subsidized housing at 200 North Dearborn Street. Although areas surrounding the Loop were beginning to support residential buildings, nobody had yet ventured into the business center of the city. After all, the Loop was named in recognition of the many transit lines that connected the commercial downtown with residential neighborhoods. With an effective commute system in place, developers had just left the Loop to business use. This was my next area.

I commissioned Jerry Olson of Hansen Realty to survey the area for me to find any available buildings for sale. The results of his search identified two vacant buildings that were owned by large corporations, but were not listed for sale. One was owned by Citigroup, and the other was owned by Ameritech.

We first looked at the property owned by Citigroup, located near the Daley Center on Dearborn Street. The site consisted of one building, approximately 150,000 square feet. This was the smaller of the two properties, and assuming this project would be the more manageable of the two, I had Jerry try to contact Citigroup to determine if they were willing to sell the building. He was able to get in touch with their real estate department, and quickly learned they weren't very motivated to sell the building. We abandoned our attempt to purchase that building, and redirected our efforts towards the Ameritech property.

212 and 230 W. Washington Street: Washington Franklin Self-Park. 183 units built from 1998-2000.

The vacant property owned by Ameritech occupied the north side of Washington Street, from Wells Street to Franklin Street. There were two 21-story office towers on the site, a two-story structure attached on the back side of one of the office towers, and a 15,000-square-foot vacant lot that was used as a park.

Ameritech also owned an adjacent 50-story office tower, on the corner of Randolph Street and Franklin Street. In the late 1980s, Ameritech built a large suburban low-rise office complex in Hoffman Estates. Over a period of years, they gradually transferred many of their employees to their new location in the suburbs.

By the time we came calling in 1998, the two 21-story towers had already been vacant for a few years. Jerry contacted Ameritech's real estate department, and was referred to their outside consultants, Equis Partners, Ameritech's advisor for all of their real estate transactions. We met with Equis, and learned that Ameritech did not have any plans for the site.

Most developers would want to demolish the buildings and start from the ground up; they would not be interested in rehabbing the existing structures. However, Ameritech wanted to preserve the two office towers because they were architectural treasures built in the early 1900s. Not only did the buildings have architectural significance, but they also had a historic feature at their roots, underneath the structure of the buildings.

One of Chicago's best-kept secrets—until 1992, that is—was the tunnel system stretching 62 miles and lying 43 feet under the city's center. This underground system, covering nearly the entire Loop, including Ameritech, had moved freight transportation and congestion away from the city streets since the early 1900s. Although its operations have nearly ceased, it still remains a unique, and sometimes troublesome, element of Chicago's character.

In 1899, the city of Chicago approved Illinois Telephone and Telegraph's—and specifically George Jackson's—plan to construct tunnels under the city. These underground rails, built roughly seven-and-a-half feet high and 6 feet wide, with walls a foot thick, were initially intended to carry the company's network of telephone cables. However, when payment issues arose, Chicago Tunnel Company eventually took over. The use of the tunnel was quickly expanded to transfer merchandise between businesses, deliver coal to multiple consumers, and distribute mail throughout the city.

Chicago Freight Tunnel System

The underground freight lines had numerous connections above ground, via elevators, where shippers could exchange merchandise and where department stores—including Marshall Field's—could receive shipments. In addition, the tunnel had two coal-receiving stations. At these locations, railroad cars, above ground, would deposit coal into bins under the track. The deposited coal was then sent down to the tunnel, via chutes, and loaded into side-dump cars. An overhead trolley would then pull the railcars to their destinations, at which point they would dump coal into a hopper below each of their twenty-two customers' boiler rooms. Over time, however—once the subway system was constructed, and once natural gas replaced coal—the underground tunnel system became less significant. Since 1973, it has been used mainly by utility companies. As of today, some of the tunnel system was never filled in and still exists as a great piece of Chicago history.

In September 1991, new pilings were driven into the Chicago River near the Kinzie Street drawbridge to prevent barges from running into the bridge. One of Chicago's best-kept secrets definitely remained a secret to the contractor at that time. The contractor accidentally drove a piling through the river bottom and into the underground tunnel system, puncturing the ceiling of the structure. What initially was a slow leak of mud turned into a flood of 250 million gallons of dirty water from the Chicago River into the remaining tunnels.

On April 13, 1992, the tunnel system that so many people were unaware of became the center of attention. The tunnel system could not contain the rush of water from the Chicago River. Multiple buildings in the Loop which were connected to the tunnel system were now flooded, some buildings had as much as 40 feet of water in their lower levels. To anyone walking through the Loop everything appeared fine; there was no water on the streets. Still, the Loop quickly became a ghost town, much like it used to be after 5 p.m., when all the middle-class workers left their jobs to go home in the suburbs.

The city was effectively shut down as officials searched for the source of the leak. It wasn't identified until Larry Langford, a reporter for WMAQ, spotted the Chicago River spinning in a circular motion, similar to water draining from a bathtub, near the Kinzie Street bridge. After numerous attempts to block the then 20-foot hole in the tunnel, workers finally clogged the source with sixty-five truckloads of rocks, cement, and old mattresses. In the end, the flood cost the city a total estimate of $1.95 billion. I am grateful I did not own the Ameritech properties on that day.

I went ahead and made an offer to Ameritech for $6.5 million to purchase the west tower, located at 212 West Washington Street and the park that was located next to it. Before they made a decision, Equis interviewed me to gauge my company, and the scope of the project I envisioned for the site. They were concerned with my ability to handle a development project of this size. They believed Ameritech would always be perceived by the public as my partner in this project, and they wanted to have full confidence in me before committing to sell the property. Equis then asked me to prepare a presentation for the Ameritech real estate department.

I was reluctant to do the presentation. To do it right, I would have to spend $10,000 to $20,000. Also, I was a little concerned that my ideas may get divulged to my competitors. No matter how confidential a meeting may be, in situations like this, the details have a way of winding up in competitors' hands. That would have instantly resulted in other developers bidding against me to purchase the property. At this point, there were no guarantees that Ameritech was going to sell to me. My offer was very low for property in the Loop. I was offering about $150 per square foot of land in the same market where a similar site at 1 North Wacker Drive had sold for $600 per square foot of land. Since I had no other choice, I agreed to do the presentation.

Hartshorne+Plunkard, the Chicago based architectural firm, was hired to prepare the design concept for the renovation. They developed a plan that converted the 21-story office tower into a 183-unit residential condo building, with retail on the first floor. They prepared all the materials I needed for my presentation, including floor plans and renderings of the project. With all of the visual materials in place, I still had to prepare what I was going to say.

My oral presentation focused on three main points. The first point was that residential condos in the Loop would create a city center, much like what was seen in New York City, London, or Hong Kong. Second, the presence of the new homeowners would attract more businesses to the area and enliven the dreary Loop environment. Finally, the rehabilitation of the building would save it from demolition and preserve the architectural heritage of the site.

The night before the presentation, I could not sleep. My points just kept running through my head. At 4 a.m., I gave up trying to sleep and got out of bed. I continued to prepare myself mentally for the presentation. I wanted to impress upon Ameritech that my plan was the best option for their site.

The panel from Ameritech's real estate department, assembled to attend my presentation, listened intently as I spoke. I covered all of my points in detail. I further reinforced that our project would preserve the architecture. One look at the facade of the building and anyone could see and feel the magic of its design. With current labor and material costs, no one could ever afford to replicate the architecture and aesthetics of the building. The primary architect for my project, Jim Plunkard, accompanied me to the meeting. Jim talked about his company and other notable projects they had designed. He shared his thoughts on how he felt this project was a cutting-edge concept for the Loop.

When our side of the presentation was complete, the head of the real estate department for Ameritech had a few questions for us. He inquired about my company's experience with renovations of loft buildings and the nature of our finances. I explained that our development experience was primarily in loft projects, so that was our specialty. In regards to our finances, I laid out the strategy we had used on all of our loft condominium developments. This project would follow the same template, but on a larger scale. Our plan was to raise $8 million in investor equity, and obtain a $35 million revolving line of credit. Up until this point, our biggest development had been Clocktower Lofts with 113 units. This project was 60% larger at 183 units.

It was hard to tell how receptive they were to my presentation. I left the meeting unsure if I had done enough to convince them my company was qualified to develop the site to their standards. Ameritech was not going to allow just anyone to do this project. Their name would always be associated with the buildings. They wanted to guarantee that I was competent as a developer before moving forward. I did everything I felt I could on my end. It was now up to them to make a decision.

One week passed before I had their decision. After that amount of time, I was sure Ameritech had sold me out, to create a bidding war on the property. It is now safe to say that I clearly did not understand their motives. There was no bidding war; I was the only buyer they were considering. Bill Tom, from Equis Partners, finally contacted me and told me that Ameritech had agreed to my offer with one condition: they would sell me the 212 West Washington Street building, and the park at Washington and Franklin Streets, for $6.5 million if I agreed to buy their other 21-story tower at 208 West Washington Street, within one year of the first closing. Without hesitation, I said yes. We only had development plans for the single tower in my original offer, but I would worry about the other building when the time came. I asked Bob Finnigan if he could get started raising equity.

The design was still in the early stages of development. The 212 building would have a lobby and retail stores on the first level. Parking would occupy levels two through five, and the condominium units would occupy levels six through twenty-one. I was tossing around a few ideas about putting some additional retail space on the Franklin Street portion of the property, along with a street access ramp to the parking levels of the building. A ramp had to be designed to provide access to the parking. The original idea was to create a spiral ramp, but I felt the contemporary look of a spiral ramp would not fit well with the architecture of the building. I suggested we find a consultant, who specialized in these issues, to help with the design. One of the engineers, working on the project, referred me to a parking consultant named John Hammerschlag.

The parking industry is a small fraternity dominated by a few companies. John Hammerschlag is considered one of the best U.S.-based parking consultants in the industry. Luckily for me, his office was located in Chicago. I hired John on an hourly basis to sit in on our design meetings and give his input. Over the course of the first few meetings, he was brought up to speed on the design of the overall project and the issues we were facing. For the first three meetings, he just absorbed information and provided no suggestions.

230 W. Washington Street: Washington Franklin Self-Park.

After the fourth meeting, however, he pulled me aside with an idea. Attached to the back side of the 212 building was a two-story structure. John pointed out that if that structure could be demolished, there would be sufficient room to build a public parking garage. The new garage could have retail on the first level and provide access to the parking levels of the 212 building for the homeowners.

We had never considered a public parking garage as a part of our project. John's idea changed everything. His solution not only solved our design problem with the access ramps, but it also included a public parking garage with additional retail space. This would truly allow us to maximize the use of the site. In an instant, John had created over $10 million of added value to the project.

The number of available parking spaces in the Loop was limited. With high demand for parking, and no way to increase the supply of spaces, public garages in the Loop had become some of the best real estate assets in the city. By suggesting the integration of the parking garage into the design of our site, John found a way to bring a new public parking operation to a market that many thought was closed to new players. I knew right away that this was one of those "holy shit moments" in real estate.

The engineers and architects adopted John's idea and began work on the new design. During a design meeting, John had another brilliant idea: a tunnel to the parking garage. The public garage could be accessed from Washington and Franklin Streets, but not from Wells Street. He observed that access to the garage from Wells Street could be provided by a tunnel that came down from the street level, and traveled through the basements of the 208 and 212 buildings to connect with the garage. Although we were under contract to buy the 208 building from Ameritech, we would not be able to implement the tunnel into the design until I officially owned the building. John's new idea expedited the timeline for the closing on the 208 building. I treated the acquisition of the 208 building as a separate project. Bob Finnigan raised a separate pool of equity to purchase the building. We purchased the building for $6.5 million, using $3 million of investor equity and financing the remaining $3.5 million through LaSalle Bank. The building appraised at over $10 million. We had no trouble securing the financing. As soon as we closed, I had an easement granted through the building for the parking garage, into perpetuity. No matter what happened with the 208 building, the Wells

Street access tunnel to the garage would always remain.

The design for the parking garage was quickly finalized. John recommended three contractors to whom we submitted the plans for bidding. He claimed that one company, in particular, James McHugh Construction, was the best. McHugh Construction was based out of Chicago, and they specialized in building concrete structures, such as parking garages, bridges, and stadiums. Performance certainly reflected price; McHugh Construction's bid was the highest at $6 million. Still, John attested that they were well worth the money, if we could afford them.

I went to LaSalle Bank, where I had my revolving line of credit, to present my plans to add the parking garage into the project. What I thought was going to be an automatic extension of credit, was not. I requested the additional funds necessary to build the garage, but they would not expand my line of credit unless I came up with additional equity. They wanted me to come up with $3 million in 30 days. I told them I could come up with $5 million in 90 days, if they would allow me to leverage my equity in the 208 building, to obtain a second mortgage for $2.5 million. LaSalle Bank gave their consent for me to get a second mortgage on the 208 building. I set off to find a lender for the second mortgage, while Bob worked on raising another $2.5 million in equity.

Throughout the years, I had developed relationships with many banks. During the 1990s, there was vast consolidation in the banking industry. Many of the local banks which I had previously done business with, were no longer in existence. The local banks were all disappearing, with the majority of them being absorbed by much larger regional banks. It used to be much easier for me to get a loan. I was a local developer, working with local banks, and the loan officers at these banks knew me personally. As the industry changed, though, I was subjected to more oversight by my lenders and had to jump through more hoops to secure financing.

Lakeview Bank was a perfect illustration of the

transformation that had occurred with local banks in Chicago. They had been locally owned until they were purchased by LaSalle Bank, a subsidiary of ABN Amro. When Lakeview Bank was acquired by LaSalle, they lost their autonomy to operate like a neighborhood bank. Instead, they were now receiving their marching orders from headquarters in Amsterdam. It was disclosed to me that executives at LaSalle were instructed to be extra cautious with their business and real estate loans, due to the exposure their parent company had faced in Asia during the Asian financial crisis in 1997 and 1998.

While searching for a bank to handle the second mortgage on the 208 building, my architect, Jim Plunkard, suggested I inquire at Bridgeview Bank. The owner of Bridgeview Bank, Peter Haleas, was a friend of Jim's. I had never met Mr. Haleas, but he was familiar with my business and my reputation, through his association with Jim. On Jim's recommendation, I contacted Bridgeview Bank and arranged to present my proposal for the second mortgage to him.

Nothing could have prepared me for the reaction I received from Mr. Haleas regarding my proposal. I launched into my proposal to him and the bank's president, Deborah Peterson and had been speaking for about 7 minutes, when he stopped me by simply saying, "Okay." I could have gone on longer. I assumed at that point that he had enough information to pass my request on to his loan committee for approval. That was not his intention. I was absolutely bewildered when he then said, "When would you like to fund this?" I was at a loss for words. I had become so accustomed to the hierarchical decisions that were required by most banks to get a loan approved. I eventually responded, "Next week will be fine."

By securing the second mortgage at Bridgeview Bank, I had half the equity I needed to expand my credit line at LaSalle Bank. The other $2.5 million was raised by Bob through the issuance of mezzanine bonds. We had never used bonds as a means of raising equity until the Clocktower Lofts project. The majority of our investors used funds from retirement plans for their investments, and could not take advantage of the tax benefits offered by real estate ownership. The bonds provided our investors with a straight return. There was no guaranteed rate of return, but the bonds could yield up to a 20% return. The bondholders received no ownership interests; we retained 100% of the ownership of the assets.

Mezzanine bonds are more commonly known as junk bonds. They are considered very risky investments. Our investors were well aware of the risks they faced with their purchase of our bonds, but many of them had invested with us in the past. They were comfortable with our track record from our previous development projects. Some of our investors had even purchased bonds in all three of our projects at the Ameritech site. Bob raised a total of $13.5 million in equity through the issuance of the bonds: $2.5 million for the parking garage, $8 million for the 212 building, and $3 million for the 208 building. As promised, LaSalle Bank then expanded our construction line of credit. Construction would begin once we had all of our permits from the City of Chicago Building Department.

One of the first things I did after we closed on the 212 building in the fall of 1997, was submit an initial set of plans for our project to the building department. I wanted to get the process of obtaining the required permits started right away. I knew the process would not be quick, but I could not get anything accomplished with the building department. My architect then hired a consultant to walk our plans through all of the different areas of the building department. This strategy did not work, either. The consultant reported that the project was so large that no inspector wanted to be responsible for signing off on the plans. Nothing happened for months. The plans for the project sat somewhere in the building department, just collecting dust.

Every day that passed, without the permits, was costing me more money. The sooner we started demolition, the sooner we could start construction. Nothing happened for months. My team and I were in limbo until we could get those permits. Something had to happen, and it had to happen fast. I finally decided I would call the mayor's chief of staff, Terry Teele, to ask for assistance in getting our construction permits.

Before Ameritech ever agreed to sell me the property, their CEO, Richard Notebaert, had sought Mayor Daley's approval. The mayor was extremely excited about our project and fully supported the idea of putting residential real estate in the Loop. He thought it would be a great development for Chicago. At the start of the development, Terry had contacted me and expressed the mayor's interest in our project. He told me if I ever needed anything, I should call him. The mayor considered it a priority to have more places for people to live in the Loop.

I explained to Mr. Teele the difficulties we were facing in trying to get our permits from the building department. He listened to what I had to say and then responded, "No problem. I will get right on this." Mr. Teele took my plans and placed a note on each portion that required separate approval from the individual areas inside the building department which said: "Any questions, see Terry Teele, Mayor's chief of staff." Thinking that the department heads would see each note and realize the mayor had an interest in this project, Mr. Teele assured me his intervention would speed along the process, and we would have our permits in no time.

Four months later, we still did not have the permits. I went back to see Mr. Teele. I told him how I was comforted by the current situation. He looked at me strangely as I continued. I told him we developers, for years, always have had problems getting permits from the building department; I was relieved to see that even the mayor's office could not get a permit from their own building department. I realize now how unorganized the department was. To defend the building department, the number of requests for permits had probably never been this high since the first major development boom from 1890 to 1920.

Mr. Teele was aggravated by the situation, too. He hesitated for a moment and then said, "You know what? Just start your demolition without a permit, and I will try to get one for you within a month or two." I was shocked that the mayor's chief of staff was giving me permission to start a 350,000 square-foot, 21-story, mid-rise project, one block from city hall, without a permit. Just to make sure I understood him correctly I said, "Are you sure I can do this?" Mr. Teele gave me the go-ahead to start demolition.

The next day, I had demolition crews working, and our project in the Loop was finally underway. Three weeks later, two inspectors who normally walked east from city hall to go to lunch, walked west that day, directly past our project on 212 West Washington Street and witnessed our crews working. They located our construction office on the first floor of the 208 building. These inspectors came in and asked my head construction manager, Jim Ridley, to see our demolition or building permits. Jim informed them that we did not have one. They in turn proceeded to write us multiple tickets for conducting demolition and construction operations without a permit.

Jim called me right away and told me what happened. I dropped what I was doing and drove straight to the work site. I gathered up the tickets and took them to Mr. Teele at his office. He looked carefully at the tickets and wrote down the names of the two inspectors who signed them. He then looked up at me and said, "Don't worry. You won't see these guys anymore." He instructed me to have my crew get back to work, and that he would take care of this on his end. We went back to work, and did not have any further problems from any inspectors.

Weeks went by, and we still did not have our permits. One day, while driving north on Franklin Street, I approached the traffic light at Washington Street. I had the habit of looking up at my building every time I drove by to assess how far the interior demolition crews had progressed. That day, as I stopped at the light, I watched two workers pulling a window out on the twentieth floor. I sat there in awe as the 4 by 8 foot sheet of glass they were removing, slipped off of the scaffolding, and floated down toward the ground like a leaf falling from a tree. I was paralyzed in my seat.

Washington Street is a major thoroughfare in the Loop. It is heavily used by both vehicular and pedestrian traffic. Thousands of people and cars travel down this street every hour. I held my breath as the glass came closer to the ground. I could tell it would fall in the middle of Washington Street, but it was not clear what it was going to hit. It felt like time stood still as I watched the scene play out.

Semi-trailer truck traffic is prohibited in the Loop until after 6 p.m. Out of nowhere, a huge semi-trailer truck appeared, driving down Washington Street as the sheet of glass was falling. It was 2 p.m., and this driver had no business in the Loop at that time of day. But I was so grateful that he was there. The glass fell harmlessly on the trailer portion of the rig, and shattered into a million little pieces. The driver never had a clue that anything had even happened. Some of the glass fragments had fallen in front of the building at 225 West Washington Street. The janitor for the building noticed the glass and promptly swept it up.

The entire event lasted no more than 90 seconds. I was jolted back to consciousness by the man in the car behind me, incessantly honking his horn. My heart was beating so hard in my chest, and I could feel a vein throbbing in my head. I pulled my car into the job site. I sat there for a moment, thinking about what might have happened had the sheet of glass fallen on a pedestrian. I was incredibly lucky that did not happen. I walked into the construction office and instructed my construction manager to stop all demolition until we had our permits.

The incident with the falling glass could have put an end to the project before it ever got started. I could not even begin to calculate the potential liability we would have faced, had someone been injured. Our liability would have been further exacerbated by the fact we were working without a permit. I did not want to consider what an accident of this magnitude would have done to my reputation, or whether there was potential for criminal liability as well. The permits finally arrived 30 days later, and our crews were able to resume the demolition process.

I vowed to myself to never start a project without a permit again, no matter how many city officials gave their approval. I should have known better in the first place. When Mr. Teele, the mayor's own chief of staff, gave me permission to start the demolition without a permit, I initially felt empowered. Had that sheet of glass fallen and injured someone on the ground, I am not so sure that Mr. Teele would have told the press that he had given me permission to work without a permit. It probably would have been a very lonely day for me. The City of Chicago would have disavowed any knowledge of my activities and denied that any prior approval was given.

The demolition process involved gutting the entire 212 building, including the removal of the windows and all interior non-bearing walls. What was left was a brick shell with concrete floors. We also demolished the two-story structure that was on the back of the 212 building to make room for the parking garage. The contractor for the parking garage began the site preparation before starting construction. They estimated it would take 12 months to build the garage from start to finish. The construction of the garage was the smoothest aspect of the entire project. James McHugh Construction exceeded my expectations. Every week I met with the foreman for an update, and his report was always the same: "Ahead of schedule and under budget, boss!" If only things had gone as well with the condominium project.

No one really knew what the costs would be to renovate a century old 21-story building, since it was not done very often. New construction afforded a contractor the ability to closely estimate his costs. Our subcontractors gave us their best estimates, but none of them allocated properly for the condition of the site. Throughout the entire project, we had to constantly renegotiate the terms of our contracts to add on the extras which were required to get the job done. We faced obstacles with materials being stolen and subcontractors not staying on schedule. Our only saving grace was that our acquisition price for the building was so economical, that we could absorb the cost overruns.

Developers rarely renovate buildings of this size. This created a completely new set of problems for our subcontractors. It became a daily challenge to move large quantities of materials and personnel up and down the freight elevator and stairways. The size of the building had a greater adverse effect on some subcontractors, more so than others. The company we had hired to install the balconies for every unit failed to perform as promised. It became obvious that the scope of this project surpassed their capabilities.

The contracting of a company for the fabrication and installation of the balconies was one of many aspects of the project. Our normal operating procedure was to request bids from at least three companies. The subcontractor we chose for this project was one we had previously worked with, and we were well aware of what it would cost to have the balconies attached to the building. I made sure to ask him if he thought the height of the building would be a problem. He assured me that his company could handle the task, and we agreed on a price that was comparable to what we had paid in the past.

In order to install the sliding glass doors for each unit, a mason came through and cut out all of the doorways. When this part of the job was complete, everything was ready for our subcontractor to begin installing the balconies. We were expecting them to be installed in the summer of 1998. Summer soon became fall and fall turned to winter. No progress had been made whatsoever. They had not even begun the assembly of the balconies at the site. When we inquired, they claimed they were assembling the balconies in their shop and when they were complete, the installation would go quickly.

They never arrived. With the advent of winter and freezing temperatures it was not a good idea to try to affix the assemblies to the exterior walls. The conditions were not ideal for that type of work. We were stuck until the weather improved. We could continue with the interior construction, but nothing was going to happen with the balconies until the warmer weather came in the spring. We could not close on any of the completed units until the balconies were in place.

The renovation of the building started from the bottom up. The major systems, plumbing, electrical, HVAC, elevators, and fire protection had to be installed first throughout the whole building. When these systems were completed, we worked our way up, floor by floor, finishing the units. Just as we did with other projects, we wanted to sell the completed condominiums as they were finished. This would allow us to pay down our revolving line of credit as the project progressed. By the time we had completed the first four levels of condos, we did not have a single balcony installed. All of these units were sold, and we were waiting on the balconies in order to close.

The contract with our subcontractor for the balconies was terminated. We found a new contractor who had experience working on mid-rise and high-rise buildings. The biggest obstacle was that the new contractor could not start until the weather broke.

We were stuck in a holding pattern with over fifty units in

inventory that we could not close on. My closeout/punch-list superintendent, Laurie Musgrave, came up with a solution. Musgrave's job was to make sure all the final touches were applied to a unit before the closeout inspector from the building department came to perform the final inspection.

Laurie designed a barricade, which was installed in front of every sliding glass door, to prevent anyone from opening the door and subsequently falling off the edge of the building. It was not an extremely elegant addition to the condos, but we hoped it would temporarily serve its purpose, and with the inspector's approval, we could start closing on the units. Laurie showed the barricade to the closeout inspector and explained the problems we had with the first contractor. It was becoming very urgent that we close on the completed units. The line of credit was not fully extended, but it was closer than I wanted it to be. The inspector agreed to sign off on the units. He presented us with certificates of substantial completion, which indicated the items that remained incomplete. It was our responsibility to complete the listed items within 60 days and report to the inspector when we were ready for the final inspection.

The closings began right away. Residents were excited to move into their new loft condominiums. The new balcony subcontractor was on site preparing the balcony assemblies for installation. He wanted to have everything ready so that when the weather improved, there would be no further delays. When spring finally arrived in 1999, they worked 12-hour days to knock out the job as quickly as possible. They maintained their pace 7 days a week for 3 months, until all 183 balconies were installed. We estimated the delay caused by our first subcontractor's failure to perform according to his contract cost the project approximately $500,000. Trying to recover this loss was pointless because the subcontractor did not have sufficient assets or insurance to cover that amount.

On large projects, it is an option to have subcontractors pay for a performance bond. We never required it because, over the years, we had developed working relationships with our subcontractors. We had no reason to believe they would fail to perform after developing such a positive track record with us. The problem could have been avoided had this subcontractor been honest with himself about his company's ability to do the job.

By May 1999, the garage was completed. James McHugh Construction was true to their word; they finished the project in less than 12 months. I was shocked when their project administrator came to see me upon completion of the garage, presenting me with a check for $60,000 as he said, "We ended up using less rebar than we had originally budgeted. Here is refund for the difference." I was absolutely astounded. I then said, "You know exactly what you are doing. Contractors don't do this. You know that I am going to tell this story for the rest of my life." That $60,000 was the best advertising money could buy. It is almost 13 years later, and I am still talking about it; James McHugh Construction is a first-class operation.

The public parking garage was an instant success when it opened in May of 1999. The 575 parking spots filled in 3 days. I am not sure if that is a record or not, but I had no idea demand was so great for parking in the Loop. By the fourth day, I wished I had made the garage a few levels higher! The retail space on the first floor of the garage was occupied by a restaurant called Cosi. They adopted a unique, French gourmet fast-food concept, which was immensely popular in the neighborhood. Cosi has remained a tenant since day one.

Rehabbing a 21-story building in the Loop, with my small management team of four people, was wearing me down mentally and physically. Being on the front line of this $100 million project was taking its toll on me. The idea of rehabbing the 208 building was rapidly losing its appeal. Every month, we were making two mortgage payments on the building, and we were nowhere close to being ready to start developing that building. I decided to list the 208 building for sale. I would have to find another developer who would agree to rehab the building. I was happy with what I had accomplished, and was content to let someone else develop the 208 building. It needed to sell fast because servicing the debt on the property was eating up our equity.

Not being sure if the 208 building would sell quickly enough, I hesitantly listed the parking garage for sale as well. It broke my heart to list the garage. I was so proud of that asset; I hated the idea of losing it. But there was not much of a choice; something had to be sold to pay down the debt. I knew the garage would get some interest from some of the larger companies that owned parking operations across the United States.

There was action on the 208 building first. Concord Homes (now Lennar Homes) offered to buy 208 West Washington Street from me for $10.6 million. We had purchased the building for $6.5 million, but we were bleeding money on the property at a rate of about $100,000 per month for the two mortgage payments, property taxes, and maintenance. At the contract price Concord was offering, there was still some room for profit. During the due diligence period, Concord withdrew their offer because they could not make the numbers work. The $10.6 million price was too high for them to develop the site, and reach the profitability level they were seeking.

Then, we got a hit on the parking garage. Equity Office, one of the largest commercial real estate investment trusts, which was run by Sam Zell, offered to buy our parking garage for $22 million. I would have preferred to keep the garage and sell the 208 building, but it was too late. Selling the garage would generate a considerable profit, which would allow me to get Concord Homes back to the table at a lower price.

Jerry Olson was the broker who was handling the sale of the 208 building. He was confident that he could get Concord to buy the building for $9.6 million. Their numbers would work better at this price point. Concord agreed to the new price. We signed a contract with a July 31, 1999 closing date. The contract stated that we had to provide access to the parking levels of the building, through both the 212 building and the parking garage. Nothing in the contract stated that this access had to be completed before the closing date.

I was relieved to rid myself of the 208 building, but I was not as excited to sell the garage. Then one day I was reading an article in the *Chicago Tribune.* It stated that Equity Office was cancelling $350 million worth of purchase contracts they had on assets like my parking garage. I sat there wondering if the contract they had with me was included in this. As far as I knew, they were still under contract with me. No one had told me otherwise. A day later my attorney contacted me to let me know that Equity Office had backed out of our contract. I was overjoyed.

Fast forward to July 31: we thought we were ready to close with Concord. It turned out that they expected the access to the parking levels of the buildings to be in place before the closing. We had understood the contract to say that the access had to be there before they started building condominiums. It didn't matter what we thought the contract said; they were not going to close until we installed the access ramps from the 212 building into the 208 building.

Concord used the issue of the access to their building as an excuse to delay the closing, in order to save money. I was sure they intended to eventually close; they just weren't ready to start their project. Why tie up $9.6 million in capital in a property that was going to sit for months while they figured out what they were going to do with it? They were going to use any means possible to postpone the closing and defer the costs associated with owning this asset. As long as I owned the building, I had to keep making the payments.

To make matters worse, Concord stipulated that they wanted us to obtain a separate permit for the access ramps we were building for them, even though they knew this was unnecessary. We already had building permits for the site. Their position was that the access ramps, connecting the 208 and 212 buildings together, were not listed on the original plans. My position was that the new ramps were part of the overall project. We would submit the designs for the ramps along with the numerous other "as built" modifications for our project to the building department when we were finished. But I really had no choice; I could not sue them because then the case would be tied up in court for months. I was going to do everything in my power to close on that building at the earliest date possible.

Concord likely thought they had bought themselves 4 to 6 months. Normally, it would take at least 3 to 4 months alone, to get the necessary permit. Instead, I hired a consulting company that specialized in expediting projects that required building department and planning commission approval. The owner of the company, Nick Fera, was a former department head in the building department. I told Nick I would pay double his fee, if he could get me the permit yesterday morning. He promised to do his best. In the meantime, I hired James McHugh Construction to come back to construct the ramps. The job consisted of cutting holes in the walls on three levels of both buildings and pouring concrete ramps at different grades to compensate for the change in elevation from one building to the other. The buildings were less than an inch apart, so the span the ramps covered was not very large. All three ramps were done in one day. Nick had the permit for me on August 28th. I contacted Concord to let them know we were ready to close.

They never expected me to get the permit and install the ramps so quickly. At the closing, they inspected the permit and pointed out that the city inspectors had not signed off on the work. I was dumbfounded. I never had an inspector sign a permit card. I did not even know there was a place for them to sign. Sure enough, when I turned over the card, there was a place for the inspector to sign. They had me again. This minor issue could have delayed the closing for weeks. I did not have weeks; this closing had been dragged out long enough.

My closeout/punch-list superintendent, Laurie Musgrave, knew most of the city inspectors well, since she worked with them regularly on our site. I asked her if she could run down to city hall and get an inspector to inspect and sign off on our ramp construction. She said that she could do better than that. She had never told me this before, but in the interest of keeping good city relations, she kept a case of Heineken beer in the refrigerator of our construction office. Apparently many of the city inspectors in the Loop would hang out in our garage at the end of their work days. They had some time to kill before they had to clock out at 4:30 p.m. at city hall.

Musgrave told me she would get the signatures. She then proceeded to block the exit to the parking garage, and track down our friendly public servants. She was not sure what level they were on, and wanted to guarantee that she would find them before they left. She was able to find them, and they gladly agreed to inspect the ramps. What normally would have taken weeks, she got accomplished in a couple of hours.

Three days later, when it was all said and done, we closed on 208 West Washington Street. Concord Homes went on to have a successful development. Most importantly to me, I was able to sell the 208 building and keep the garage. Our development project at 212 West Washington Street continued into the summer of 2000. The units did not sell as quickly as they did in Bucktown, but we eventually sold them all.

Ameritech took a chance on me. They were well aware that they had sold the property to me well below market price. But they thought that the consumer would always associate Ameritech with the development of this project, even though it was not the truth. Ameritech needed me to be successful. By selling the property to me below market price, they were helping to ensure my success. If I had failed, the public relations damage to their reputation was far greater than a few million dollars added to the sales price. The price offered to me was an insurance policy that the project would be a success for all.

Summary

Expand Your Team When Necessary

The realm of parking garages was new territory for us. Adding John Hammerschlag to our team as a consultant was one of the smartest business decisions we ever made. His ideas on the parking garage design created the best development project of my life. Before Hammerschlag joined our team, I wasn't convinced that the architects could effectively overcome the design problems we were facing. Turning to an expert in the parking industry was the only logical decision. I had no way of knowing how much value he would bring to the partnership. The pivotal moment came when I realized that we needed help. Had I not made this decision, we might have settled for a substandard design. Hammerschlag brought experience and perspective that was missing from my team. He has become one of my most trusted advisors.

Protect Yourself

In today's litigious society, it is even more important to take precautions and have the necessary insurance coverage. Do not take shortcuts in business. The mayor's chief of staff, approving the start of my demolition without a permit, struck a feeling of empowerment in me at the time. I quickly learned that it was a mistake to act on. Who would have protected me had someone been seriously injured when the sheet of glass fell from that 20th-story window? A businessman needs to be able to foresee future possible outcomes of various scenarios, and plan accordingly to protect his company from liability.

Global Forces Can Affect Local Business

ABN Amro's irrational concern over my Ameritech project highlighted how their problems in Asia in 1997 could affect the day-to-day operations of my project in Chicago: business does not operate in a vacuum. There are countless global forces that can affect local business. In most instances, it happens indirectly, but in my case, the bank that we had borrowed money from was part of a global conglomerate that had worldwide exposure. It is a businessman's responsibility to understand the global economy and how it can affect local business.

Understand the Limitations of Contractors

As a real estate developer, I worked with numerous contractors throughout the years. I enjoyed seeing our contractors experience success alongside of our success. The Ameritech project was our biggest project to date. It was the first time we had ever renovated a multi-story mid-rise in the city. The scope of the project was more than one of our contractors could handle. It was my responsibility to assess our contractor's ability to get the job done. I did not discover the extent of my contractor's limitations until it was too late. This project was too big for this particular contractor, and its failure cost us thousands of dollars and delayed our closings by months. I should have made sure before hiring them that they had the requisite experience on projects of this size.

Draft Ironclad Contracts

The contracts that we use for both sales and purchases of real estate have evolved over the years. The results are the product of thousands of dollars in legal fees and countless transactions. What started off as relatively simple has become more involved, as our business has grown, and our deals have become increasingly more complex. I would like to think that we have planned for all contingencies in our contracts, but it is hard to know until a contract provision is challenged. It was not our contract, but an issue that was not specifically addressed in the contract, that created a problem for us when we were selling the 208 West Washington Street property. I incorrectly assumed that our buyer would not require the installation of the ramps that connected the parking levels until their condominiums neared completion. They used this issue as an excuse to postpone the closing until the ramps were installed. We should have outlined our responsibilities, in regard to the ramps, more clearly in the contract. Drafting an ironclad contract that left no issue unaddressed would have prevented many headaches.

Chapter 8

I'd Rather Be Lucky Than Smart

General Fire Extinguisher: 2002–2004

During the summer of 2002, Rodger Chenore, a broker with Paine Wetzel, brought a fantastic deal to me. He had discovered a 12-acre site on Shermer Road in Northbrook, Illinois, that was occupied by General Fire Extinguisher. The company had just undergone Chapter 11 reorganization. As part of their reorganization, they wanted to sell their property to raise the capital they desperately needed. They would then lease back the property from the new owner. I agreed to buy the site for $2 million.

Northbrook lies just north of Chicago, within the upscale North Shore community. Buying property in this location for less than $4 per square foot was a steal. General Fire Extinguisher agreed to pay $200,000 per year, on a triple net basis, to lease back the property. They were responsible for all costs associated with the building, including the real estate taxes. The lease guaranteed me a 10% annual rate of return on my investment. Although the tenant and the building were both of poor quality, I was captivated by this prime piece of land in the center of Northbrook. If General Fire Extinguisher ended up going out of business, this location would be ideal for the headquarters of any major corporation.

I closed on the property and looked forward to the cash flow this asset was going to generate. I had decided to do this deal alone. I put up $700,000 and financed the rest through LaSalle Bank. When General Fire Extinguisher had emerged from Chapter 11, I thought they had made the necessary changes to their company in order to continue as a going concern. Apparently, they did not.

Eight days later, they filed Chapter 7 bankruptcy. They never recovered. General Fire Extinguisher dissolved their corporation, and I was left with a building on a 12-acre site that had little to no adaptive reuse for another tenant.

I know I have said this before, but constantly revising a business plan has been a recurrent theme in my life. Life is all about plan B. Here, I thought I was being prudent, doing this deal alone; so much for my guaranteed 10% return. Now, instead of having all the cash flow to myself, I faced all the exposure alone.

I had to remind myself that the property was still a fantastic deal. As an industrial site, it was easily worth double what I paid. It would be worth even more as residential, but I was not sure the community would go for it. The situation called for me to implement plan B a little sooner than I had originally planned.

I called Chenore and told him what had happened. He agreed to list the property for me. I had him list the property for sale or for lease. I was willing to build a new corporate facility and lease it to a new company, or I could sell the site as is to a new buyer. Several months passed without any interest in the property. My banker at LaSalle Bank, Mike McGrogan, was starting to become concerned. Without a tenant, he was worried I would not be able to maintain the loan for the property. Neither of us expected the tenant to vanish. I assured him that I had the situation under control.

The zoning on the site restricted its use to industrial or commercial tenants, but this site was attracting no interest from the business community. The General Fire Extinguisher property, even while they were in operation, was an eyesore in Northbrook. It was absolutely out of place. It was bordered by a golf course on one side and by single-family homes on the other. I believed it would have been an ideal location for residential housing. I never imagined there were people in Northbrook who agreed with me. Usually, someone had to convince a community that development was a good idea. In Northbrook, their city council recognized they needed to encourage development before it was ever suggested to them.

Out of nowhere, an article appeared in the newspaper reporting that the Village of Northbrook was considering allowing zoning for denser condominium and townhome uses in the Shermer Avenue Industrial Corridor. They realized that there were few places for couples, wanting to downsize, to relocate in their city, once their children had moved out. These empty-nesters were instead moving to other communities that offered condominium and townhome properties. The Northbrook City Council wanted to prevent any further loss of these residents, and changing the zoning in this corridor was a way to encourage residential development to accommodate the changing needs of the community.

Literally overnight, without any effort on my part, I received four separate offers to purchase the General Fire Extinguisher property. Each of the four offers was contingent on zoning. Zoning is never a foregone conclusion. I needed to identify the buyer who I believed was most capable of getting the zoning approved. If I selected the wrong buyer and they were unable to secure the zoning, I would be back at square one; it was important for me to get this right the first time around. Obtaining zoning is never a speedy process, and in the meantime, I had to keep making the mortgage payment on a property that was not generating any cash flow. The selection of the buyer could make or break this deal.

All four of the offers were in the $4 million to $4.5 million range. The bidders were all top-quality builders with good reputations, who were all willing to match the top bid. To me, price was secondary. I wanted to choose the builder most politically familiar with Northbrook. North Shore communities had a tendency to be difficult to navigate regarding zoning matters, and I needed a builder who could really get the job done.

While evaluating the offers, I received a call from Brian Hoffman of Red Seal Development. Red Seal was a small local company based in Northbrook and had been developing homes there since the 1950s. Hoffman had left me a message boldly stating that he believed he was the only developer that could get the zoning changed on the property. The other bidders were all major, national, residential developers with no local ties to the community. Hoffman was very persistent with his calls. I started to think that Red Seal Development might be the perfect developer for the site.

We arranged a meeting at Red Seal's offices in Northbrook. After meeting Hoffman and seeing his company, I was convinced they were my buyer. I felt very comfortable with Hoffman's ability to get the zoning change. We signed a contract for $4.5 million, subject to receiving the proper zoning for their project and the satisfactory completion of due diligence.

General Fire Extinguisher had used a wide variety of chemicals in their operation; thus, there were some environmental concerns. The environmental standards for residential land were more stringent than industrial land. This site could be reused as industrial or office space with no remediation, but for residential use, the environmental condition of the land had to be investigated. Red Seal hired an environmental consultant to assess the extent of the contamination of the site. Toxic material was discovered in the soil in some areas of the site, and would require a large remediation. This involved extending a clay cap over the affected areas, which could not be breached and was required to always remain intact. Red Seal agreed to install the cap at their own cost, which exceeded $1 million.

The second hurdle was the zoning board. This was setting up to be a fight. We soon discovered that the decision to encourage multi-family developments in the community was not unanimous. I noticed that the sentiment was much like what we experienced when we tried to get property zoned for the Wrightwood Court Townhome development: most people fear change. With the development on the cusp of becoming a reality, people came out of the woodwork to oppose the project. The difference between the DePaul community of the 1980s and Northbrook in 2003 was that

North Shore residents were sophisticated, wealthy and able to hire lawyers to fight any builder.

Today, DePaul has the same demographics as Northbrook, maybe slightly wealthier. In the 1980s, DePaul was dealing with old, dilapidated structures and transient residents. The changes we developers brought to that community were needed. In Northbrook, however, the changes were more optional. The community was already well-established. They did not necessarily need more development to attract residents to their city; they needed development to retain the ones they had.

The battle began between the factions in the Northbrook community. On one side was the group that saw change as necessary, and on the other side was the group that feared change. The zoning war continued daily. Hoffman worked with all parties and addressed each of their concerns. In the meetings with the zoning board and the neighbors, he answered all of their questions in a professional and patient manner. I attended many of those meetings, and I did not envy Hoffman's task.

After 6 long months, the zoning board approved the rezoning for Red Seal's project at the General Fire Extinguisher site. No other developer could have obtained that zoning change. It would have been impossible for an outsider to come into Northbrook and convince the opposition that the development was good for the community. Hoffman used his insider status as a bargaining chip. Northbrook was his home as well, and he truly only wanted what was best for it.

With the zoning approved and the environmental issues dealt with, there was nothing barring us from closing on the deal with Red Seal Development. There were no modifications to the contract; we closed for the agreed upon amount of $4.5 million. When I purchased the property, I thought I was being smart by locking in a 10% rate of return. I ended up being lucky. I stumbled upon one of the best returns on capital in my career. Even with the additional cost of the monthly mortgage payment for 18 months, the return on my equity was over 250%. This was one instance in which I'd rather be lucky than smart.

Red Seal Development went on to build a beautiful condominium and townhome development, which was a great addition to the Northbrook community. There was considerable demand for their product from the empty-nesters in Northbrook and other neighboring communities. The development was a success for everyone involved. It took a leap of faith on the part of the community to permit the development to go forward, but I believe that Northbrook is better off today for having put their faith in one of their own: Brian Hoffman and Red Seal Development. I could not have been more pleased with the results.

Summary

Have a Plan B, and Don't Panic

When General Fire Extinguisher went bankrupt for the second time, days after my closing on the property, it caused a bit of panic on my part. In a moment's notice, what I thought was going to be an easy-going cash flow property, became a forced development project. This situation exposed me to greater risk and required me to spend a considerable amount of time to create a new strategy. I had to come up with a plan B.

Plan B surfaced when, out of the blue, an article appeared in the newspaper saying that the City of Northbrook was considering allowing empty-nester development on my site. This created a new possible path to success. I knew the property was well located and it was relatively inexpensive, so in this case, buying right kept my options open.

Evaluate Offers Thoroughly

After receiving many offers on my property once it became public knowledge that the City of Northbrook would consider a residential development at that location, I chose Red Seal Development because they had the best history of rezoning property in Northbrook. They were smaller and less financially capable than the other companies that had bid on the property, but they had the advantage of understanding this local niche market of wealthy North Shore consumers. I was an outsider in the community, and I was aware that it would take an insider's expertise to get zoning approved for a residential development. Red Seal Development also understood the environmental challenges the site posed, and had the necessary resources to remedy the situation. All of these factors played into my decision to select a local developer over a national company.

The politics involved in getting a property rezoned in Northbrook were intense. Had Red Seal Development mishandled any part of the rezoning, the whole deal could have collapsed. I had tried to market the site for industrial or office use, with no success. If the rezoning had not come through, returning to this path would have been much harder, and probably would have resulted in less profit or even could have failed altogether. The success of this deal provided me the reassurance that I had backed the best horse in the race.

Chapter 9

Family Matters

The Pillars: 2001–2004

With my years of construction experience, it was only natural that I would serve as general contractor for the construction of my own home. I did it once in 1986, when I built a home in South Barrington, Illinois, but I was not really excited to do it again. When we started searching for a second home on a lake, I wanted to find one that did not require any renovations. I dealt with construction Monday through Friday. I deserved a break from it on the weekends.

When I was a young boy, my family would vacation at different lakes in Michigan and Indiana. My two sisters and I all enjoyed being in and around the water, and my dad taught the three of us to water ski, pulling us behind a small boat that had a 10hp motor.

In 2001, my son was 14 years old and growing up fast. I wanted to find a home on a lake where I could share the same experiences with my son, as my father had with me.

One day that summer, together with my wife, Marla, and my son, Loren, we drove to Fontana, Wisconsin, to have lunch at the Abbey Hotel on Lake Geneva. After lunch, we walked up a path that led from the hotel toward a line of homes on the water. At the top of a hill stood a stately, white, frame house with four large ionic columns that grabbed our attention. The facade of the house had a historic, Greek Revival look. The houses on Lake Geneva all faced the lake with their back sides to the road. My wife noticed that this house had a "For Sale" sign. We wrote down the number and returned to the hotel.

As soon as we got back to the hotel, we called the broker and told her we were interested in seeing the house. The broker agreed to meet us at the property and show it to us. She gave us a tour of this 100-year-old home, and told us it was locally known as "The Pillars" because of the 14-foot-tall,

2-foot-thick columns that were visible from the lake side. We fell in love with the exterior design of the home, but as a contractor, I knew this home needed a lot of work. The floor sloped 5 inches from one side of the house to the other, and doorknobs fell off when you pulled on them. I had promised myself I would not do any personal rehab projects.

"The Pillars": Second home on Lake Geneva, Fontana, Wisconsin. Built in 1900, and rehabbed in 2001.

The listed price for The Pillars was $1.3 million. That seemed a little steep, even for Lake Geneva. After our tour, we went to the broker's office and I made an offer of $1.1 million. I could see that both my wife and son were very excited about the prospect of owning this house. I had to admit, I was becoming committed to the idea, too. The next day, the owner countered my offer, and we eventually settled on the price of $1.2 million. The closing date was set for July 15th, so the owner and his family could enjoy the home for the first part of the summer before they sold it.

We enjoyed the home for the rest of the summer. By September, my wife had plans to renovate the interior of the entire house. I told her that I personally did not want to do the work; this was supposed to be a getaway destination for me. Of course, I was somewhat compromised; I hired a former employee of mine, who had started his own construction company, to do the job. I was listed as the general contractor, but Teddy Rywak oversaw the day-to-day operations of the project.

The house was over 4,000 square feet. The project wasn't any different from any of the historic rehabs we did in DePaul—the inside was totally gutted and all that remained was the exterior shell. During the demolition, we found several copies of the *Chicago Daily Tribune* from May 1900, between the hardwood floor and the structural sub floor. It was obvious that they were placed there on purpose. Using the space between the flooring as a time capsule, the papers were preserved in excellent condition. I carefully removed them, and had these pieces of history further preserved behind glass, in frames. In one of the papers, an advertisement read: "Mail Order Cocaine $1.00. First Order Free." Apparently, cocaine was legal in 1900, and advertisers already knew what it would take to get their customers hooked and coming back for more.

The most amazing discovery of the renovation project was the natural talent my wife had for design. She directed the construction crew as they rebuilt this historical treasure every step of the way. They widened hallways, added skylights, and brought out the best features that this 100-year-old home had to offer. From start to finish, the project took about 9 months. When the construction was complete, Marla focused her efforts on the interior design.

I feared the cost of this phase of the project. Many designers would spend $400,000 to $500,000 on furnishings, fixtures, and other accoutrements on a project of this magnitude. Interior design can become so customized that it only has inherent value to the current owner. Upon resale, the owner is forced to discount the sales price because many buyers will want a design scheme that fits their personal tastes. I was wary of that route, so Marla developed a design that was less personal and more compatible with the exterior Greek Revival architecture. The best part about it was that she did it all for under $100,000. The look of the finished product far surpassed anything a professional designer could have achieved with twice the budget.

I was pleased with the outcome. This was supposed to be a vacation home, but I could not help but think of it as an investment, too. The improvements added value to the property that I felt exceeded our cost basis. I didn't know how long we would keep The Pillars, but I wanted to spend as much time with my family there, while my son was still young. I knew that once he got older, he would move on to college and not want to spend his summer weekends with mom and dad.

The community of Fontana, Wisconsin was relatively small, so everyone was familiar with The Pillars. It was one of the most unique homes on Lake Geneva. After the renovation was completed, we began to receive visits from curious area real estate brokers who wanted to tour the home. The house created a lot of buzz in the community. There is also a public walking path that went around the entire lake and right through our back yard. People would stop along the path and admire the properties along the lake. Everyone was usually very friendly and polite. On occasion, we would become engaged in conversation with people on the path who inquired about the renovation project.

Word traveled quickly. Marla was approached by real estate brokers to see if she was interested in renovating and decorating other homes on the lake. These homes around Lake Geneva were all beautiful on the outside, but the interiors, from a design and decorating standpoint, were out of date. I quickly shot down the idea of buying, restoring, and reselling million-dollar homes. It was an area of real estate in which I did not want to venture. But I do believe that if anyone could have done it and made money at it, it would have been Marla.

We spent our summers, and sometimes Christmas, at The Pillars through 2004. My son graduated from high school that year, and was accepted to the University of Wisconsin in Madison, where he also made the crew team. The University of Wisconsin had one of the top crew programs in the United States and had produced Olympic athletes. Between school and crew, I knew that lazy summers at Lake Geneva were over for all of us. Around the same time, I partnered with Alpine Confections to purchase the Fannie May candy company. My company would own only the real estate portion of Fannie May, and Alpine would own the candy operation, leasing the locations they planned to keep open back from us. I needed equity to help cover my portion of the deal. With my son taking courses that summer, and training on campus with the crew team, I decided to put The Pillars up for sale. When my son found out I was selling the house, he was very upset. He envisioned that The Pillars would always be in our family. In 3 short years, we had created many happy memories from our time there. I had $1.8 million invested in the purchase, renovation, and interior design of the house. We listed the property for $2.4 million. It sold in 9 days for $2.25 million.

Selling a multi-million-dollar home usually takes months or even years. I believe our success was attributable to Marla's sharp design and interior decorating. The buyer took one look at the house and he knew he had to have it. He didn't want us to remove anything; he wanted the total package, from the towels in the bathroom to the dishes in the kitchen cabinets. Everything went together perfectly to make The Pillars what it was.

One hundred years from now, whomever owns The Pillars may consider renovating it again for the second time in two centuries. If they do, when they pull up the floorboards, they will find our time capsule that we placed there. We wanted to hold true to the spirit of the original tradesmen who built The Pillars in 1900. They had to know they were part of something special, because there is no other home like it on Lake Geneva.

Summary

Early in my career, all I could think about was achieving financial success. Having this drive wasn't a bad thing, but I was worried that my son was growing up fast, and that he would soon be off to college and beyond. Life is too short, and I knew I needed to be spending as much time as possible with the people who mattered most: my family. The balance between business and family may be the hardest thing to manage in life. On one hand, I wanted to provide the best life possible for my family. On the other hand, I wanted to spend as much time as possible with my family.

Rehabbing the 100-year-old Pillars brought out the amazing interior design talent my wife possessed. This skill made The Pillars a wonderful place to live and ensured its resale value. Selling a custom home like The Pillars within 9 days of it being listed is a feat in and of itself. It just demonstrates the extraordinary work that my wife put into the project, giving the house its unique appeal. My wife naturally mastered a talent for making a dollar spent on the rehab and interior design look like $1.50. I stress this concept repeatedly with architects in my business; mastering this skill has infinite value to a real estate business.

Chapter 10

The Best Retail Corners

Fannie May: 2004

Founded in 1920 by H. Teller Archibald, Fannie May is one of the most recognizable brand names in the candy industry. The company began with its first retail location at 11 North LaSalle Street in Chicago. For years, Fannie May regaled generations of customers with their premium candies made from only the highest quality ingredients. In 1992, the company was sold to a private equity group that expanded Fannie May to 197 locations in malls and shopping centers across the U.S. Thirty-one of their stores were in company-owned, freestanding buildings, occupying some of the best retail corners in their respective cities.

Fannie May's parent company, Archibald Candy, filed for bankruptcy protection in June 2002. Heavily in debt, the company, after a restructuring, was able to emerge from bankruptcy, only to default on its obligations within months. In early 2003, Archibald Candy again filed for bankruptcy protection. This time, a decision was made to sell their businesses as a means of satisfying their creditors. Archibald Candy was the parent company of multiple candy companies, and the manufacturing operations for all of their candy businesses were based in Chicago. As a part of the bankruptcy proceedings, the individual candy businesses were to be sold at auction to the highest bidder. The manufacturing facility was being sold separately outside of the auction. I had read about the bankruptcy in the newspaper, and although I was not interested in the candy operations, I was very interested in acquiring the Fannie May real estate holdings.

The manufacturing facility was listed for sale by a broker I knew well, Vern Schultz of Colliers, Bennett and Kahnweiler. I contacted Vern to see if he could help me get an inside track on the bidding for the real estate portion of Fannie May. Vern did one better than that; he put me in touch with Alpine Confections, a company that would be bidding at the auction. Vern thought that I would have a better chance at getting Fannie May's thirty-one freestanding stores if I partnered with Alpine who was primarily interested in the candy operation.

Alpine Confections was not what would be considered a large company for the industry. They were based in Salt Lake City, Utah, and the company was run by two entrepreneurs, Taz Murray and David Taiclet. Both had brilliant business minds, but they lacked the capital they needed to purchase Fannie May on their own. They were in a delicate situation. They saw the freestanding stores as essential to the success of the Fannie May brand. Many of these locations had been serving customers for decades, and had helped establish Fannie May as the iconic candy brand that it is today. Murray and Taiclet needed a real estate partner, with whom they could pool their resources, to increase their odds of getting the winning bid for the company.

I met with Murray and Taiclet, and expressed my interest in purchasing Fannie May's real estate portfolio. We struck a deal the day before the auction. If we were successful, I would own the thirty-one freestanding stores and Alpine would own the candy business. Alpine would select the stores they wished to reopen as Fannie May retail locations, and I would have the freedom to do whatever I wanted with the remaining locations. At the auction, we would bid as one. We signed an agreement within 24 hours of meeting. My attorney, Michael O'Connor of Fuchs & Roselli, worked with their attorney, Josh Agrons of Fulbright & Jaworski, into the early morning hours on the day of the auction, to finalize the agreement. Everything was in place, just in time for the auction. Had I waited another day to contact them, I would have missed the auction completely.

The auction was being conducted by a Chicago law firm, Jenner & Block. According to the U.S. Bankruptcy Code, they were mandated to take into consideration the best interests of all involved parties in the liquidation of Archibald Candy's candy businesses. To do this, Jenner & Block planned to auction each of the thirty-one freestanding Fannie May stores, individually, and then together as a package. Similarly, the Fannie May candy operation would be auctioned separately, then together with the real estate holdings. The goal was to determine which bid, or combination of bids, would yield the best price for the Fannie May assets.

The auction started with the bidding on the individual thirty-one freestanding stores. The winning bids ranged from $200,000 to $1.2 million. The joy of having the winning bid on a single property was short lived, when the entire real estate portfolio was auctioned off for $14.5 million. The winning bid on the real estate portfolio exceeded the total of the individual thirty-one winning bids.

The bidding continued on with the candy operation. We sat back and watched the bidding. Alpine had no intention to bid on the parts. They didn't want the company without the stores. The candy operation was bid up to $18.5 million by a large candy company. Seeing the results allowed us to analyze our numbers and revise our bidding range. At this point, I privately informed Alpine that I was willing to increase my contribution for the real estate from $14 million to $16 million. This would give them more room to work with while bidding. The auctioneer called for a break before the bidding began on Fannie May's combined assets in one complete package.

It was common knowledge amongst the other bidders that Alpine was the stalking-horse bidder. They had been distributing Fannie May products throughout the bankruptcy. During the break, one of the other bidders, who had become perplexed by Alpine's inaction, asked the auctioneer why Alpine was not bidding. The auctioneer responded, "I don't know," then directed his attention to the table at which we were sitting and said, "Alpine, why aren't you bidding?" Josh Agrons, Alpine's attorney, stood up and addressed the auctioneer, "Sir, not bidding is not bidding." The room, occupied with nearly 200 people, erupted into laughter. Alpine clearly had a plan, and it was not going to be divulged to anyone until the last minute.

I knew what the plan was. We were waiting patiently to bid on the entire company, real estate included. After the break, everyone prepared for the final stage of the auction. The purpose of this final bidding was to determine if one bidder would pay more for the complete package, than for the sum of all the parts. The bidding started at $33 million, which was the total of the two winning bids for the candy business and the real estate. Alpine was in the final bidding for the combined assets with only two other companies. The bidding quickly surpassed $36 million in increments of $300,000. One of the two other bidders dropped out, leaving just Alpine and a much larger competitor in the running. The other company had ten times the revenue and financial power as Alpine. The bidding continued back and forth until Alpine had the high bid at $38.3 million. The other company asked for a short break. After a 15-minute break, they came back with a bid of $38.6 million. Now, it was Alpine's turn to ask for a break.

Murray and Taiclet conferred with their attorneys. They had nearly reached the absolute maximum they could afford to bid. Once again, they looked at me, and I told them that I could not go any higher. They decided to make one last bid. When the auction resumed, Alpine placed their final bid of $38.9 million. If they won, they would be responsible for $22.9 million, and I would be responsible for $16 million. After what seemed like hours, but was probably only seconds, the other bidder informed the auctioneer that they would not be making any further bids. The auction was over. Alpine had won ownership of the Fannie May candy company and its thirty-one retail locations.

I had committed $16 million to the purchase price of the company for the real estate. The deal did not close for 30 days, during which time I raised $7 million in equity from investors, and obtained a $9 million loan from LaSalle Bank. I was surprised at how quickly the financing all came together. We closed on the properties on schedule. Mike O'Connor suggested that we name the real estate partnership O.L.B., in reference to the "one last bid" that took the prize. There could not be a more appropriate name for the partnership.

The closing occurred in April 2004. Alpine was on a strict timeline to reopen the Fannie May retail stores: they wanted to be up and running by October 2004, just in time for the holiday season. Alpine chose to lease nineteen of the thirty-one stores back from us. The remaining sites were available to be rented out in whatever manner we saw fit. The geographical locations of the stores created a new problem for us: how to manage thirty-one individual properties in six different states from our offices in Chicago.

My Chicago management staff was limited to one highly talented property manager. I always prided myself by running a small to medium-sized firm with only a handful of capable employees, or outside consultants. Upon buying the Fannie May stores, I now had small retail sites in Illinois, Indiana, Michigan, Virginia, New Jersey, and Pennsylvania. My staff could handle the states in our immediate vicinity, but not the rest. I couldn't afford to station a manager on the east coast, nor was it cost-effective for someone from Chicago to fly to a site when a problem arose. I needed to find a solution fast.

As I thought about how to solve this problem, I remember reading about Frank Cuneo. Cuneo was a Chicago real estate and print baron of the early 1900s who often employed the ground lease, or today, an absolute net lease. The purpose of this unique tool is to place the complete burden of the real estate on the tenant. It doesn't matter what happens, if the roof falls in, windows are broken, or the grass needs to be cut—all structural work and maintenance becomes the responsibility of the tenant. Cuneo used 99-year ground leases as a way to maintain his name in the chain of title into perpetuity. For Cuneo, the thrill of a ground lease was to live beyond the grave, through his property assets. For me, the thrill was to transfer all responsibility to the tenant.

I consulted with the brokers I was using to lease the properties, Paul Bryant, Peter Scannell, and Dan Tausk, of Mid America Real Estate, about using a ground lease. In order for a tenant to be willing to sign a ground lease, the location has to be superior, and the tenant has to be financially stable enough to take on the added responsibilities. The tenants would be responsible for maintaining the structure and all common elements of the property. It's a more expensive lease option for the tenant than the typical triple net lease. Mid America agreed that the Fannie May sites were of such quality that offering a ground lease would work.

Mid America marketed the remaining twelve locations. The sites attracted many Class A tenants. Within a year, we had leased the majority of the properties to a variety of restaurants, banks, and cellular telephone stores. Many of the tenants renovated the buildings to fit their needs. We wanted to find tenants who were willing to make capital improvements to the property, because the more money a tenant has invested in the property, the less likely they are going to walk away. Any company investing $250,000 in capital improvements to my building is going to make a good tenant. If they don't pay their rent, they can be evicted, and all the improvements are left behind.

The beauty of the ground lease was highlighted in two specific cases of mine: TCF Bank in Wood Dale, Illinois, and Ramada Hotel in Grand Rapids, Michigan. In both cases, our tenants demolished the former Fannie May store that was on the site. TCF Bank constructed a $3 million building where our building once stood. Knowing that if they went out of business, and they couldn't take the building with them, TCF Bank was willing to sign a 30-year lease for $150,000 a year. They have no plans of going anywhere anytime soon.

The Ramada Hotel was in a more precarious situation. They owned the adjacent property to ours and wanted to build a new hotel there. According to the zoning, they needed to provide a certain number of parking spaces for the size of the hotel they were building. They didn't have enough land of their own, so they had to lease the space from us. What used to be a Fannie May store in Grand Rapids is now part of a parking lot for Ramada. They signed a 30-year lease with us. If for some odd reason they fail to meet the terms of the lease, they could be evicted from our property. The fate of the hotel would then be in jeopardy, because they would be in violation of the zoning ordinance.

Usually, the larger the capital investment a tenant makes, the longer the lease term is. A tenant that makes a serious investment in the property is going to pay their rent. They also favor a long-term lease, so that they have sufficient time to ensure a return on their investment, and to write off the associated costs. Further, a tenant doesn't want to sink a lot of money into a location they are renting, only to have the landlord not renew their lease after 5 years. The tenant then wants to lock in a longer lease to prevent that from happening.

The process of getting Fannie May back up and running was not exactly smooth for Alpine. After the closing, they received a CD-ROM of all the Fannie May recipes. The disc had been kept in a bank vault for safe keeping until it was turned over to Alpine at the closing. These recipes were the most valuable assets Fannie May had. After reviewing the recipes in preparation to start production, it was discovered by an officer from the old company, who had been retained by Alpine, that there was something very wrong with the recipe for Fannie May's famous Pixies. This caused a momentary panic. Alpine had just paid $22.9 million for these recipes, and something was not right. Luckily for them, this officer happened to have the correct recipe in his head. It was a good thing they kept him around.

In October 2004, candy connoisseurs lined the sidewalks to shop at the newly reopened Fannie May stores. Within the first year, a total of forty-five stores were opened, including the nineteen sites they were leasing back from us. Their success can be attributed to Taz Murray and David Taiclet's savvy business tactics, and to customer loyalty to the Fannie May brand. In 2006, Alpine went on to sell Fannie May along with some of their other brands for $85 million to 1-800-Flowers.com. The Fannie May brand continues to be successful, and I am pleased to have them as first-class tenants in our first-class sites.

Purchasing a company's assets in bankruptcy proceedings can have unpredictable results. I don't think any of the other bidders at the auction really knew the true value of the real estate. I ended up paying $16 million for the real estate portfolio, but I knew it was worth more. In 2004, we estimated the value to be more in the neighborhood of $24 million. We did get a bargain, but we had to assume the risk. The risk with acquiring assets from a bankrupt company is always higher, which is why it is so important to buy them at a low price. It's difficult to know exactly what is being bought until months after the closing. The only defense against the unknown factors from a bankruptcy is to pay the lowest price possible.

Taz Murray and David Taiclet are visionary businessmen who saw value in a bankrupt candy company and brought it back from the grave. Being able to see value where others see obstacles is what makes all the difference in business.

Summary

The Last 5% Is 95% of the Work

Having the perseverance and work ethic to see a vision through to the end is what made these guys special. It's guys like Taz Murray and David Taiclet who are capable of doing the last 5% that it takes to make a business truly successful. The last 5% of a deal is 95% of the work.

Business Contacts Add Value

The value of networking is fully revealed in the success from my partnership with Taz Murray and David Taiclet. I would have never been introduced to them had it not been for Vern Schultz. Vern was the conduit that made this deal possible for me. My success can be attributed as much to the people who have helped put me in the right place at the right time, as it can to my business acumen.

Chapter 11

Real Estate as a Commodity

Current River Farms, Arkansas: 2008

In 1996, I had purchased a historic office building with my partner, Bob Finnigan, and a CPA, Leonard Metzl. We leased the first floor and kept the second floor for ourselves to create a shared office area. Each of us had our own business interests as well as common business interests. For the most part, we all worked together, but for our own separate companies. In the early 2000s, a young CPA, Brian Savage, joined Metzl's accounting firm, and thus became a daily presence in my life.

I didn't really pay attention to Brian for the first year that he worked in our office. He was about 30 years old, and I didn't give him the time of day. What could someone his age possibly have to offer? As time went by, I would have brief conversations with him, only trying to be polite. Over time, however, when I really started listening to what he had to say, I realized maybe he did have something to offer. Slowly, our brief conversations evolved into nearly two-hour lunches. Brian had a finely tuned sense of the changes occurring in the world of commodities. Every conversation produced intellectual stimulation, and each day, my appreciation for him and his insight grew.

Brian opened my business mind to the world of commodities. I was still focused heavily on real estate in Chicago, and I had never before considered investing in commodities. But he introduced me to authors like Jim Rogers, the author of *Hot Commodities,* and to investment newsletters from the likes of Doug Casey and Marc Faber. These men all extolled the new virtues of commodities. The market forces of supply and demand were driving commodity prices to all-time highs.

It was only a few years earlier in 2000 when oil was $11 a barrel and gold was trading for $250 per ounce. Brian challenged me to find a way to invest in commodities.

Investing in commodities can be as simple as buying stock in a company that produces the commodity of interest. If I wanted to invest in oil, I could buy ExxonMobil. If I wanted to invest in metals like uranium, copper, iron, silver, gold, lead, or zinc, I could invest in a mining company like Rio Tinto. A complicated way to invest in commodities involves the futures market. The futures market allows speculators to purchase large quantities of a commodity using leverage, with the amount of leverage differentiating depending on the commodity. Speculators acquire contracts to buy or sell a specific commodity at a future date. The underlying idea is that the speculator sells his position at a profit before the contract delivery date.

The futures market didn't appeal to me. With leverage, gains were magnified when a trade won, and likewise, losses were magnified when a trade lost. The risk was not worth it to me. Besides, if I was going to invest in something, I wanted to own assets. Brian told me that he had started investing in small Canadian oil and mining companies in 2002. He began with $15,000 in a brokerage account. By the time I was considering investing in commodities, he had already more than doubled his money. Brian had a natural ability at finding innate value in these small companies. They were all penny stocks listed on either the Vancouver or the Toronto stock exchanges. He had done his homework on these companies, ensuring they were not fraudulently overvalued, before ever deciding to invest.

One day, Brian ran into my office and started talking about a company, Silvercorp. It was a Canadian mining company listed on the Vancouver Stock Exchange. The company was run by Dr. Rui Feng, a Chinese businessman with a Ph.D. in geology. Dr. Feng had been in Canada for years, teaching mining at a university, and he had recently begun to buy silver, lead, and zinc mines from the Chinese government, in the area north of Kunshan and west of Beijing. Brian believed that out of all of the ugly ducklings he had reviewed, Silvercorp might be the home run of the group.

I was initially concerned, knowing that a lot of small mining operations never get off the ground. There are many challenges that are too great for them to overcome. Dr. Feng had an advantage: he was familiar with China, where he was purchasing mining assets, and he spoke the language. He also had access to qualified personnel from his years of teaching. As there is a serious shortage of qualified mining engineers worldwide, one of the hardest parts of starting a mining business is finding qualified employees. He had yet another advantage here, and the investment was starting to gain appeal.

Brian continued to explain that Silvercorp had a Canadian 43101 appraisal that indicated that there was rich concentrations of silver, lead, and zinc, per metric ton of soil, in their mines. As Brian listed off all of the positive characteristics of the company, my concerns were alleviated. After further research, Silvercorp was starting to sound like it could be a good investment. The opportunity to research Silvercorp, as well as other mining companies, was coming up in February 2005 at a mining convention in Vancouver, Canada. Savage suggested I attend the convention where I would have the opportunity to meet Dr. Feng.

I discussed the convention with my wife, and she agreed to accompany me to Vancouver. If the convention was a bust, we would still have a nice weekend alone in a city neither of us had ever visited. Still, I was looking forward to learning more about the mining industry. Even if Silvercorp did not pan out as an investment, there was a chance I would find other companies that were more attractive.

Before leaving for Vancouver, I went ahead and purchased 100,000 shares of Silvercorp. I resolved to evaluate the company at the convention, either liquidate or increase my position upon returning home, depending on how I felt about the stock. I had called the company's investor relations department, informed them that I would be in attendance at the convention, and would like the opportunity to meet Dr. Feng.

I was surprised at how mild the weather was in Vancouver compared to what we were used to in February in Chicago. When we landed, it was in the fifties and rainy. The hotel where we were staying was attached to the convention center, with a view of the bay. After checking in, we headed straight for the convention. I was immediately fascinated by all of the start-up companies looking to mine everything from uranium to gold, in all corners of the world. They were all there for the same reason: to try to get private investors for their company.

Many of the other companies at the convention looked interesting, but I focused my attention on Silvercorp since Brian had spent so much time investigating this company. It was my job to determine if they really were going to be a home run.

We found the Silvercorp booth at the convention without difficulty. I had never before invested in stocks, but my strategy was to treat this investment just like any of my other investments. I invested in the projects of other real estate developers in Chicago because I believed in the project, but more importantly, I believed in the man behind the project. I wanted to have the same faith in the man directing Silvercorp, so it was imperative that I meet Dr. Feng. He was not at the booth when we arrived. We spoke to one of the company's investor relations representatives, who said she had been expecting us. We were invited to attend a special dinner with Dr. Feng that evening, to celebrate the Chinese New Year.

As I was leaving the booth, I realized that Silvercorp, unlike the other companies at the convention, was not really pushing their company. It seemed odd. I thought the whole idea of the convention was to attract private investors. Maybe they knew they had something that didn't need to be sold, something that would sell itself. I considered this as we headed back to the hotel to rest before getting ready for the dinner party.

Silvercorp had reserved a banquet room on the second floor of a Chinese restaurant. My wife and I were seated at the head table with Dr. Feng. It was a fun night, participating in the festivities of the Chinese New Year. The sales pitch that did not occur at their booth on the convention floor, occurred here, at the dinner with a select group of investors. The woman in charge of investor relations sold her heart out to those in attendance. I watched Dr. Feng the whole night as he quietly listened to people tell their stories, but he spoke very little. He did not try to sell anyone on his company. At one point during dinner, he surreptitiously told me that if he could buy back every outstanding share in his company, he would. If he wanted to buy back every outstanding share in his company, then that could mean only one thing: he was fully aware of the tremendous potential of his mining company.

In real estate, every once in a while, I had come across a deal that I knew was a home run. In those instances, the same exact thought that Dr. Feng had shared with me would cross my mind: I would wish that I could buy back the shares of a partnership from my investors. I always had to remind myself that many of my investors had been with me through the good times and in the bad times. They deserved the good times as much as I did. From the few elusive comments I received from Dr. Feng that night at dinner, I determined that he was a serious businessman with an authentic pedigree, who was positioning his company to prepare for the good times that were coming.

When I returned from Vancouver, I increased my position to 300,000 shares. I told everyone in the office to buy as much Silvercorp as they could afford. We all bought in around $3 per share. Within 6 months, the stock reached $8, where it remained for a few more months until topping out at around

$20. I had sold all of my shares at $8. My investment in Silvercorp was my first real foray into stocks, so I did not sufficiently prepare an exit strategy for the investment. Selling at $8 dollars gave me a $1.5 million profit, but had I planned accordingly, I might have held the investment at least one year to receive the preferential long-term capital gains tax rate. The plan would have forced me to hold on to the stock longer, subsequently sell it when the price was higher, and pay a smaller percentage of tax on capital gains.

Still, I was very happy with the profit I made on Silvercorp. When I find high-growth assets, whether they are real estate assets in Chicago or silver mines in China, I try to take a healthy profit out in the middle of an explosive growth phase. No one can exactly time the top or the bottom of a stock, and neither can they fault the wisdom of selling at a profit. It is easy to analyze a transaction years later and say what I should have done, but I am content with the results from my investment in Silvercorp.

I learned that being a passive investor wasn't much fun, even when I made money. It was not as stimulating as actively operating a business, but I still continued to invest in stocks. Brian and I identified eight more mining and energy companies in which to invest. I tried to make it more fun by traveling to places, like Mexico, to investigate different mining operations. We had many successful investments, but I really was looking for a way to enter the commodities market with an actual business of my own. Investing passively in other people's companies is profitable, but I wanted to find a commodity-producing business in which I could get involved as an owner.

In 2006, I started researching the ethanol business. Corn, the main ingredient in ethanol, had averaged $2.25 per bushel for the previous 40 years. I thought that an ethanol plant would be a good investment. It would capitalize on the excess supplies of corn that were keeping prices so low and help relieve some of the demand our country had for foreign oil. I enlisted the help of John Kutsch, a products engineer, to analyze the design and costs associated with building an ethanol plant. He helped me with my due diligence, and together, we embarked on a year-long quest to understand the ethanol industry.

Located on the Illinois River, south of Joliet, in the middle of corn country, I had found an ideal location for an ethanol plant. The site was as perfect as any that could have been designed. The property had access to both the river and a railroad, which would enable barge and rail traffic for delivery of corn to the plant. Tapping the Kinder Morgan natural gas pipeline, located on the property, would easily provide power to the plant. With a refinery within miles from the property, transportation of the finished product could be accomplished through a pipeline from the plant to the refinery. We really thought we were on to something great. The pieces were falling into place perfectly.

The closer my vision for an ethanol plant came to becoming a reality, the more I realized I needed to start having discussions with potential investors. A project of this size would require a significant capital investment. It would take a combination of investor equity and bank financing to get this deal done. I had discussed my idea with a few people who were interested in becoming investors, but the time was fast approaching when I would need to secure financing. The 80-million-gallon plant I was planning to build would cost approximately $75 million dollars. I had prepared reports outlining the estimated costs for the land, plant, and soft costs to present to a bank to obtain financing.

I contacted one of the top banks in the country that handled ethanol plant financing, located in Omaha, Nebraska. Before I got too far, I needed to know what kind of interest rate to expect, and how much investor equity would be required. If they didn't agree with my projected revenue and expenses, which were essential to making the debt payments, they would not even consider financing the deal.

While reviewing my projections, the bank officer told me that the price I had used to budget for corn was too low. I tried to explain that the amount I had used, $2.25 per bushel, was the average for the previous 40 years. He understood completely; however, he told me how, in recent years, they had watched the vast ethanol industry develop, and were convinced that it was going to increase the demand for corn, thus driving prices higher. There was no doubt in his mind that a more realistic estimate for corn would be $3.50 per bushel. The banker would not consider my proposal with my figures. He jokingly asked me, "Do you know the golden rule?" I responded, "No." He smiled as he stated, "Well the golden rule is: We have the gold, and you follow the rules."

I went back and reran my numbers with corn at $3.50 a bushel and it made the projected profitability look very tight for the ethanol plant. As I was questioning the viability of this ethanol plant, I couldn't help but think about the banker's projection for corn prices. What did that mean for the price of farm land? I started to back away from the ethanol plant investment idea. It was an industry that had to buy corn as a commodity and then convert it into ethanol. If the price of corn went higher, then it would only make ethanol that much more expensive to produce. I needed to be on the front end of the production process, and the best way to do that was to buy a farm and grow some corn.

It is unbelievable how my journey into the world of commodities had taken me from investing in companies that produce commodities, to considering the construction of an ethanol plant that required extensive amounts of corn, to contemplating the purchase of a farm. Buying a farm sounded a lot like real estate, something about which I knew a few things. When it came to urban real estate, I considered myself a pro, but I knew virtually nothing about rural farmland. I became a quick study as I researched farmland around the country, all the way from Montana to Louisiana.

A wheat farm in North Dakota or Montana, where average

annual rainfall was less than 18 inches, might sell for $300 per acre. Conversely, a good Iowa or Illinois corn farm, where average rainfall was up to 35 inches and soil conditions were superior, might go for $4,000 to $7,000 per acre. In the South, across Arkansas, Mississippi, and Louisiana, a rice, cotton, corn, or soybean farm could sell for $1,500 to $4,000 per acre, depending on whether the land had been precision land leveled. Farmland in the South would get 50 inches or more of rainfall, but it was not evenly distributed across the growing season. Land leveling then optimized the fields for irrigation by using satellite-based software to create a slight pitch to the land.

Land leveling was essential in the South where rainfall was often sporadic. A farm may receive a deluge of rain in the spring and then very little throughout the summer. In addition to the pitch to the field, the land leveling created distinct furrows that facilitated the irrigation of crops at root level. A farmer could run water from a river or aquifer across one end of a field, and it would slowly spread across the field to the other side. This irrigation process efficiently dispersed the water at the base of the plants. Unlike standard irrigation methods, this method employed less equipment, and also reduced the chance of evaporation that was common with sprinkler systems.

Farmers were no different than city folk. They, too, demanded the best schools for their children. A farm that was located in a good school district went for more than a farm in a lesser school district. It was the same story in urban markets in and around Chicago. Quality schools drove up the value of real estate. Soil quality was another driver of price on farmland. Farms in Iowa and Illinois sold for more than farms in Arkansas or Louisiana, because the better soil resulted in a higher expected yield.

On a daily basis, my knowledge of farming was growing exponentially. I discovered that comparable yields could be achieved in the South through the use of more fertilizer and proper irrigation techniques. My focus then shifted to purchasing a farm with decent soil and access to a plentiful water source. There were areas in Mississippi and Arkansas that appeared to meet my requirements. I believed that buying a farm in one of these two states, at half the price of a farm in Illinois, would more than offset the additional cost required to get the same yield. I contacted a farm management firm, seeking a referral for a consultant to assist me in the identification of the perfect farm to buy. They directed me to Terry Browning, a former National Security Agency employee, who had developed the technology that uses global positioning satellite to precision land level farmland.

I contacted Terry, and he agreed to meet me at a farm in Mississippi that I had identified as a potential investment. After meeting with him, I realized that I still had a lot to learn about farming. The farm was selling for $1,500 per acre, unleveled. Terry quickly assessed the farm. The soil was bad, the water level in the aquifer was falling, and the school district was marginal. He helped me understand not only what I should look for in a farm from my perspective as an investor, but also from the perspective of the farmer I would have to attract to work the land. It would be difficult to make this farm a top producer. Farmers would be hard pressed to come here, even if we did land level the property.

After this, I wanted Terry to work as my consultant, even though working as a consultant for investors seeking farmland was not really his business. He had sold the rights to the software he developed for land leveling. He primarily worked as an independent field designer for large farming operations that wished to have their fields precision land leveled. Still, I believed his experience in agriculture fully qualified him for what I needed. I proposed that I could hire him on an hourly basis as a consultant, or on a commission basis as an advisor, to locate a farm for me. Terry promised to consider my offer and get back to me.

While I waited for a response from Terry Browning, I conducted my own research on him. I called Prudential Agricultural Investments Company in Memphis, Tennessee, who had initially recommended Terry. I spoke to an executive in their Farm Management Division, and told him I wanted to know more about Terry Browning. They had utilized his services to land level farms under their control. He gave me a fascinating account of what they knew of Terry's career with the NSA. In the 1980s, he was one of a small group of individuals who possessed knowledge and expertise in using state-of-the-art satellite technology. He worked as a specialist with the NSA, tracking notorious, dictatorial, world leaders. Through the use of high-tech satellites, he would capture the radio phone conversations of people like Saddam Hussein and Muammar Gaddafi, and would then pass the intercepted communications on to the language department for translation.

Terry Browning left the NSA in the 1990s and returned to his childhood home in Jonesboro, Arkansas. Once home, he noticed that farmers were land leveling their farms with surveyor's equipment and benchmark sticks. With his experience, he was confident he could improve land leveling techniques by using GPS satellite signals. Today, most everyone is familiar with GPS technology, but 20 years ago it was a different story. Few people were qualified like Terry to take on such a radical concept.

After months of development, he unveiled a custom, hardware/software solution that revolutionized precision land leveling. The system used a GPS receiver, attached to a vehicle, to effortlessly collect thousands of land elevation points throughout a farmer's fields. As soon as this process was complete, the data was downloaded to a computer and was compiled by the software he had developed. The software would then produce detailed information about the fields, which would help the farmers determine the most efficient way to engage in their land leveling. His method was more accurate, less expensive, and simply easier to conduct.

After discovering all of this information about him, my offer to employ him as a consultant seemed so ironic. I looked like I needed him more than he needed me.

After 3 long weeks, Terry finally called and accepted my offer. He agreed to help me find a farm, through his contacts, in the South. He warned me to be patient because good farms did not come on the market very often. Instead, farms usually remained in families for generations. A farm that we would desire might only become available in the event of divorce or death. Still, I was elated to have Terry working for me, and excited at the prospect of moving forward with the purchase of a farm.

I tried to be patient. From the summer of 2007 to early 2008, I didn't hear much from Terry, and I started to lose my excitement. Real estate was doing well, and I sold some of my urban industrial buildings to raise equity in anticipation of my eventual purchase of a farm. Then one day in the summer of 2008, Terry called and informed me that he had found a 1,200-acre farm in northeastern Arkansas that was for sale. The owner was a friend of his who happened to be getting divorced, and he needed to sell. It was a beautiful rice farm that had three-and-a-half miles of frontage on the Current River. Terry implored me to come as soon as possible and see the farm.

The next day, my son and I traveled to Jonesboro, where we were greeted by Terry at the airport. The farm was located in Randolph County, Arkansas, about 40 miles north of Jonesboro. As we drove to the farm, Terry passionately detailed all of the characteristics that made this farm so ideal, and one of the best in the area. It had fantastic access to water, the land was precision land leveled and the soils were above average. It was also located in a great school district. The farm met every requirement Terry had said was so essential for a successful farming operation.

As we toured the farm, I could see it was impeccably well kept. The property was approximately one half mile wide by 4 miles long. There were much larger farms in the area, but I was in awe at the sheer size of this one. The land spanned an area that was five times greater than the area that encompassed the Loop in downtown Chicago. There was no house, barn, or other outbuildings. The only structures on the farm were four grain silos, with a total capacity of nearly 200,000 bushels. There was almost enough space to store a whole season's crop in its entirety. Our last stop on the tour, as the sun was setting, was a small sandy area along the shore of the Current River.

The frontage along the Current River was the farm's greatest asset. Water is one of the most essential elements in farming, especially rice farming. This river provided 100% of the water for the irrigation of all the fields. I was expecting to see murky, muddy water that is common in rivers across the South, but the Current River was shockingly clear and pristine. The water, coming from an aquifer that surfaces in southern Missouri, was as clear as you might find flowing from a Canadian mountain stream. The water remains crystal clear as it flows south through the farm, eventually joining the Black River near Pocahontas, Arkansas. By the time the Black River connects with the White River in Newport, Arkansas, this clear water becomes completely muddy.

From where we were standing on the shore, the beginnings of the foothills to the Ozark Mountains were visible, just to the west. We stood there, watching the sunset, looking out over the rice fields. It was one of the most beautiful sunsets I had ever seen. The humidity rising out of the fields put a translucent haze between us and the sun, giving it the most splendid yellow-raspberry color. I was sold.

The seller's asking price was $3,200 per acre. Terry told me that other farmers would jump at the chance to buy this farm, at that price. I was totally relying on him for his guidance in selecting a farm. Based on the financial statements we were provided, I calculated that I could expect between a 5% and 7% return on investment annually. I had built up a lot of capital since the mid 1990s, and I wanted to find a safe investment to protect my equity. This farm appeared to be able to serve that purpose. I agreed to pay the seller's asking price.

The seller accepted my offer. We settled on a November closing date, to give him the opportunity to close out the 2008 growing season. The seller was actually a retired farmer who leased out this land to a tenant farmer. By purchasing the farm, I inherited both the tenant and the lease. The lease stipulated that the tenant would farm the land and pay me, the owner, 25% of the gross income. I would also be responsible to reimburse the tenant for 25% of the fertilizer costs, and upon termination, I would be responsible for a percentage of the annual land leveling expenses going back to 2006. It was not the best lease to inherit, but I did not want to let it prevent me from purchasing this farm.

We closed on the property in November, on schedule. The farm was primarily a rice farm, but it also had corn and soybeans. In the fall of 2008, rice sold for around $11.00 per hundred weight, corn was about $3.25 per bushel, and soybeans went for over $10.00 per bushel. In the fall of 2011, commodity prices were much higher. Rice sold as high as $19.00 per hundred weight, corn was as high as $7.60 per bushel, and soybeans sold for over $14.00 per bushel. The cover of the September 5, 2011 issue of *Time* reads: "If You Want to Be Rich, Be a Farmer." I have watched this trend in recent years: as the value of my urban real estate has fallen, the value of my farm has continued to rise.

A commodity is an economic good. I see farmland as a commodity. Real estate in the form of farmland is fundamental in the production of agricultural goods.

After signing the contract to buy my farm in August 2008, my partner and I received an offer from someone wanting to buy our parking garage in downtown Chicago, at a premium price. I would have used my share of the profits from this deal to purchase more farms in Arkansas, but the deal did not happen. Our buyers could not get financing to purchase the garage. Their lender was AIG and little did we know at the time, but by October, the United States government would own AIG, to save it from bankruptcy.

In 2009, I purchased an additional 180 acres from a farmer whose property bordered my farm on three sides, and rested up against the Current River on the fourth side. Buying this farm gave me a total of three-and-a-half miles of frontage on the river. Since then, I have not been actively seeking other farms for purchase, but I definitely would entertain the idea if Terry Browning called again with an asset of the same quality as Current River Farms. To this day, Current River Farms is the best asset I own.

I learned that I do not have to have all the answers; I just have to be able to find the people who do. The people that I have found, while seeking investment opportunities in commodities, have made the experience truly remarkable. The counsel and friendships I have received from and developed with Brian Savage, John Kutsch, and Terry Browning have been priceless. I know that all three are always ready and willing to provide information and advice in their respective areas of expertise.

Summary

Heed to the Wisdom of Youth

You never know where opportunity will emerge. Sometimes, a great deal will be a hard asset like real estate; sometimes an opportunity will appear as a person. Brian Savage was 20 years younger than me. In the early 2000s, when it was clearly a contrarian idea to common wisdom, he was talking about investing in commodities. Recognizing these counter-trends early is key, even when the messenger is a 33-year-old kid.

Research Is Essential

Research is essential to understanding a stock asset like Silvercorp. Brian's research of the company's accounting and mining claims, combined with my hands on time with their CEO, gave us an edge. At this same time, there were hundreds of start-up companies in the mining industry, and today, all but a few have failed. Buying a stock on a hot tip or other financial gossip is a bad idea. Original research and thought is the best route to take before investing in any asset.

Information Is King

Investigating the viability of an ethanol plant led me to owning Current River Farms. The bank's forecast of the price of corn going from $2.25 to $3.50 per bushel increased the risk of an ethanol plant, but opened me up to the idea that a farm may be the asset class that I should consider.

View Real Estate as a Commodity

Current River Farms was real estate of a different sort. The energy was leaving urban real estate, but the farm put me in the middle of the commodity-based world we live in. Simply put, today I feel the best asset I own is this 1,400-acre farm in Arkansas, as I witness my urban real estate assets trending downward.

Chapter 12

Of Railroads and My Personal Derailment

Galewood Yards: 2001–2009

As work was winding down with the Ameritech project in 2001, I was contacted by a broker who said he had a 50-acre parcel of land that was located on the northwest side of the city. By this time, I had been working in Chicago for over 20 years and felt very familiar with the city. I knew of no other location that large, on the north side, that had yet to be developed. The broker informed me that the vacant land was located just north of the intersection of Central Avenue and Bloomingdale Avenue, a former railroad yard commonly known as Galewood Yards.

Galewood Yards had been an intermodal yard for many different railroad companies during the 1900s. Intermodal yards are depots used by railroads to transfer freight from one mode of transportation to another. At this particular location, goods were transferred from rail cars to trucks and vice versa. Over the years, however, the railroads outgrew this facility, and were forced to relocate to sites that had more available land. This property was later acquired by a railroad real estate company, CMC Heartland. When the property was brought to my attention, CMC was in the process of liquidating all of their assets and discontinuing operations; Galewood Yards was one of their final transactions.

I visited the property on my own, trying to visualize how it could be developed. It was zoned M1-2 which was a general manufacturing zoning that would permit many industrial uses. I initially envisioned developing an industrial corridor on the site. I believed that this location could be a good investment for my company. We were accustomed to paying up to $10 per square foot for industrial land. This deal would allow us to acquire 50 acres for about a third of the going rate. I contacted CMC Heartland directly, and offered them $7.5 million for the property.

CMC Heartland accepted my offer, and we signed a

contract with a September 8th closing date. I had 90 days to complete due diligence on the property. The due diligence period gave me time to evaluate the deal, and determine if any changes needed to be made to the contract. During that period, as fortune would have it, I happened upon an article in a local business journal, *Crain's Chicago Business*. The article described a transaction in which Metra Rail Service had purchased a 20-acre parcel from CMC Heartland for $2.50 per square foot. This land was contiguous to the parcel we had under contract for $3.50 per square foot.

I rushed into the offices of CMC to show them the inconsistency of the prices and demanded our contract price be lowered to $2.50 per square foot. CMC agreed to the contract modification and the new price of $5.5 million. It goes to show you that it pays to be diligent. Reading that one article saved me $2 million on this deal.

We closed on the deal on August 3, 2000. One week later, we were approached by Union Pacific Railroad. Union Pacific had been interested in Galewood Yards before we even purchased it. They had wanted to use the site, as it was, as an intermodal yard to better service the Chicago freight market. But they wanted to get the city's approval for their operation before they purchased the land. After our closing, CMC referred Union Pacific to us. Union Pacific offered to lease the entire property with an option to buy, once they were able to obtain the city's approval for their intermodal operation. We arranged a deal in which they would pay $825,000 per year, to lease the entire site.

In late 2001, I received a call from Mary Bonome from the City of Chicago Planning Department. She explained the city's vision for Galewood Yards. They believed that this 50-acre parcel on the north side was such a prime location, that it could only entertain the best industrial uses. They wanted operations that could create hundreds of manufacturing jobs in the city, and were not interested in any residential real estate development at that location. She knew that my company, North Development, had been involved in many residential developments, and stated that the city would not consider a zoning change on the property.

Galewood Yards Development Site: 50-acre site east and west of 1900 N. Central Ave. consisting of a union training facility, theater and residential housing.

I explained to Ms. Bonome that we weren't interested in a zoning change at Galewood Yards. We had already secured Union Pacific as a tenant. They were using the site for freight container storage, which fit within the existing zoning. Union Pacific was planning to expand their use at the site, once they received approval from the city and Mayor Daley.

Union Pacific brought great fanfare in lobbying Mayor Daley and the City of Chicago in an attempt to get approval for their proposed intermodal yard. Their efforts failed to come to fruition. The mayor rejected their proposal. The proposed Union Pacific intermodal yard would have only created seventeen new jobs for the city, and the powers-that-be had much higher hopes for this site. They would only support proposals that would guarantee hundreds of jobs on this last vacant, north side, urban parcel. Union Pacific's proposed use of the property complied with the zoning that was already in place. They didn't need the city's approval; they merely wanted it. They were unwilling to move forward with their intermodal expansion project without the city on board.

*****

The City of Chicago Department of Transportation (CDOT) began plans in early 2002 to replace the Central Avenue Bridge, which was elevated 25 feet off the ground and ran north and south, bisecting the Galewood Yards site. CDOT determined that the bridge was no longer safe for automobile traffic and needed to be demolished and rebuilt. When we purchased the Galewood Yards property, we also purchased all the land underneath the bridge as part of the deal. CDOT wanted to acquire this land to correct this oversight that must have occurred decades ago, when the original bridge was built.

CDOT proposed a deal in which we would give them the land directly under the bridge and two additional parcels on each side of Central Avenue, to be used for access ramps. This proposal would provide the much needed access to our property. As lack of access was one of the biggest problems with the site, the deal was definitely in our best interest. At that time, the only way into the area was by a small frontage road on the west side of Central Avenue. By providing improved access, the new bridge and the access ramps would add value to our property.

However, the construction of the bridge would block the dock area of a neighboring manufacturing operation. CDOT needed to buy 20,000 square feet of additional land to create a new dock area for them. We agreed to sell CDOT the land they needed for $200,000, and donate approximately 3 acres under the bridge for the ramps. We tried to be as cooperative as possible with CDOT because we supported the plan for the new bridge and access ramps.

The bridge was a project of CDOT, but it was being paid for using Illinois FIRST funds that had been set aside for infrastructure projects across the state. They budgeted approximately $22 million for the entire project, factoring in both ramps. The project was being managed by Bob Loomis, a design engineer with CDOT. He kept me updated on all developments related to the Central Avenue bridge project.

Construction was scheduled to start in early 2003.

In October 2002, Bob Loomis informed me that his boss, Stan Ketterback, was having contractors bid on the west access ramp separately as an option. This would give them the opportunity to decide if they wanted to build the bridge with both ramps, or with only the east access ramp, after they had collected all of the bids. I was under the impression that the site was going to receive both ramps. But Bob Loomis told me that when I agreed to the design, the west access ramp was always considered an option. I felt like I had gone out of my way to accommodate them, then at the last minute, they were telling me I might not get both access ramps.

I thought about the problem for a few days, and decided to call Congressman Luis Gutierrez to seek his advice. I had known Luis for about 6 years by then, and I considered him a good friend. I figured he could give me some direction on how to go about solving this problem. Luis met me for lunch at Club Lucky, a small restaurant in Chicago. After listening carefully to my situation, he did not promise or suggest any solutions. He simply told me that he would check into the situation. I walked away from that lunch, not feeling very encouraged. I still had a little time because we had not closed on the land deal with CDOT. CDOT wanted to keep the closing open-ended until they finalized their bidding process. Ultimately, if I didn't like the deal, I didn't have to close. They wouldn't have been able to move forward with the project if they didn't own the land. They would have had to go to court to get rights to the land through eminent domain.

Just before Christmas, I received a call from Bob Loomis. He was calling to wish me a Merry Christmas and let me know that I was receiving a special gift: the west access ramp. He did not give me any details except that his boss, Stan Ketterback, was screaming and pissed off. Obviously, Stan wasn't on board with this decision. So where did it come from? I was happy with the news, but I didn't know who to thank.

I called Congressman Gutierrez right away, to see if he had anything to do with what had happened. He explained to me that after our lunch he got in touch with Miguel d'Escoto, the commissioner of CDOT, and told him about my situation. Luis didn't notify me because he never received a definite answer from Commissioner d'Escoto. The commissioner promised to study the problem and discuss it with Stan. I had never met Commissioner d'Escoto, so I wouldn't recognize him if I passed him on the street. Apparently after studying the problem, he agreed that the intersection required both an east and a west access ramp. This was a very important decision for the Galewood Yards property. I thanked Luis for his intervention. He assured me that it was the right thing to do for the city.

We closed on the land with CDOT in January 2003. They promptly started work on the bridge and finished the project in early 2004. I had found out that each ramp cost approximately $1.8 million to build, so I assumed Stan Ketterback was so upset because this was a substantial amount of money. He could have possibly wanted to redirect these funds to another project that might have been over budget. I never found out what his plans had been for these funds.

The whole situation was so surreal. I had the mayor and the city planning department pushing me to develop an industrial corridor on one hand; on the other hand, I had CDOT giving me the run-around on the ramps that would be essential to developing a successful industrial corridor. Neither hand had a clue as to what the other hand was doing. In the end, we got the ramps, but it would have been so much easier to have everyone working toward a common goal.

Union Pacific leased the entire Galewood Yards property, from September 2001 to September 2003, for container storage only, after having given up on the intermodal idea. They renewed the lease in 2003 for just half of the property. They were scaling back their operations at that site, and didn't require the whole property. In 2004, Union Pacific gave us notice that they were phasing out their freight container storage at Galewood Yards, so they would not be renewing their lease. They consolidated their container storage at their primary intermodal yard in Stone Park, Illinois.

When we were leasing half the site to Union Pacific, we were still generating a 9% rate of return for our investors. We weren't under much pressure to do anything with the property while we had a tenant in place. Union Pacific could have stayed for as long as they wanted. The city might have had their own plans for the site, but as long as Union Pacific was there, we were in no hurry to get started on any new development projects. The situation changed quickly once Union Pacific left.

We were simultaneously marketing the property, for development as an industrial corridor, while Union Pacific occupied the site. We retained Rodger Chenore, a real estate broker from Paine Wetzel, to market the property. The plan was to develop the land into small 5,000 to 10,000-square-foot, boutique, industrial sites. We wanted to create a concept similar to the more centrally located Fulton Carroll Industrial Corridor in the city. It was clear that the location of our site was inferior due to the lack of access to a major interstate or expressway. The new bridge and access ramps improved access to site, but the location still lacked access to a major thoroughfare. We felt we could compensate tenants by offering new facilities with lower rents, to offset any inconvenience created by the less-than-ideal location.

After 4 years, it became evident that this marketing strategy was not going to work. We did not secure a single tenant for the industrial corridor development. The city planning department would send us potential tenants who already had manufacturing operations in the city. Our site could not even compete with their older, existing facilities. When Union Pacific vacated the property, we were left without a tenant to pay rent. Still, we had a $3 million mortgage and a $150,000 annual real estate tax bill to pay, and we were starting to get pressure from our investors to make something happen.

The land continued to remain vacant through 2005, when we finally decided to modify our strategy. I needed to convince the city planning department that their dream of an industrial corridor at Galewood Yards was unrealistic. My plan was to hire the best appraisal firm, which was also highly respected by the City of Chicago Planning Department, to plead my case. Appraisal Research Counselors was perfect for the job. Their firm was very well known and had completed many projects for the city. I explained the challenges of the site, asked them to do an appraisal of the property, and determine its best use. They accepted the assignment.

Appraisal Research would not have accepted the job if they didn't think it was a worthwhile cause. They would never take on a project that could potentially tarnish their reputation; they were one of the most respected firms in their profession in Chicago. It was not in their best interests to go against Mayor Daley and the city planning department, but it was the right thing to do. Appraisal Research found that other retail, commercial, and possibly, residential uses should be considered for the site. They concluded that a vacant site, in the urban market twenty-five blocks from any major expressway with minimal truck routes, should be converted into mixed retail, commercial, and residential zoning.

I arranged a meeting at the city planning department to deliver the appraisal. I wasn't asking them for a zoning change; I only wanted to share with them the findings of the report and attempt to get them to consider a zoning change. They weren't very receptive to our presentation. Appraisal Research Counselors provided a very thorough, measured analysis of the property, but it didn't matter. The planning department wouldn't budge from their position. My next course of action was to appeal directly to the mayor, to see if I could enlighten him to the error of his thinking about Galewood Yards.

I never had much luck getting a private audience with Mayor Daley. I couldn't even get him to return my phone calls; how did I think I could get him to meet with me? The mayor probably didn't have time for me, but I knew someone he would make time for. I called Congressman Gutierrez to ask if he could try to arrange a meeting with Mayor Daley. The mayor was able to find some time, just before Christmas 2005, to meet with us. The meeting lasted about 15 minutes. We did all of the talking, and I presented him with a copy of the report from Appraisal Research Counselors. He thanked us for coming in, wished us a Merry Christmas, and told us he would look over the report and get back to us. We never heard from the mayor.

There was no interest in the site until early 2005, when we were contacted by Wal-Mart. They wanted to purchase 15 acres of our land for a new Sam's Club location, if we were able to get the necessary zoning. We agreed to the deal and signed a contract that was contingent on zoning approval. This would have been a great deal for our partnership. After selling the 15 acres to Wal-Mart, we would have had about 35 acres left free and clear. But it was not to be.

In another part of Chicago, Wal-Mart was trying to get approval for their first store in the city, at the corner of Kostner and North Avenue. At a zoning committee meeting, the chairman, Alderman William Banks, informed the committee that he needed to table Wal-Mart's petition for zoning. Wal-Mart was a non-union operation, and this didn't sit too well for some people, so he claimed. Alderman Banks said that he wanted to review Wal-Mart's hiring practices to see if they were a good fit for the neighborhood. Alderman Bank's decision enraged the local community. It was clear he was trying to appease his constituents by supporting union operations. The community came out en masse, and presented a signed petition with over 1,500 names in favor of the new Wal-Mart store to the city zoning committee.

Over 300 members from the community showed up at the meeting to show their support of the project. Six different speakers took turns explaining that they weren't concerned Wal-Mart was not a union operation. In their community, they did not have the luxury of choosing between a union and a non-union job. They simply needed jobs. They also desired the convenience and affordability that shopping at Wal-Mart provided, which was very lacking in the city. The Wal-Mart zoning issue was instantly returned to the table, and it was voted on that day. It passed with overwhelming support. Wal-Mart went forward with that location; incidentally, they cancelled their plans for a south side location at the Ryerson Steel site and for the Sam's Club at our Galewood Yards site.

We were very disappointed when Wal-Mart informed us they were withdrawing their offer on our property. Wal-Mart was very concerned with public opinion and negative press, therefore, they did not want to get involved in any more battles with the city over zoning. Alderman Banks ruined our deal with Wal-Mart, and any other business with Wal-Mart in Chicago, for years to come. I am sure he thought he was truly representing the sentiment of the community, but didn't realize that there would be such a great public opposition to his stance. Now we had to start all over again.

In late 2005, our brokers, Mid America, introduced Kerasotes Theaters as a potential buyer for 10 acres of the site. This wasn't quite the size of deal we were looking for, because it wasn't big enough to plan our development around. Not to mention, we still didn't have the necessary zoning. We agreed to sell Kerasotes the parcel they wanted contingent on our obtaining rezoning for the property. We really didn't have a plan in place on how we were going to obtain the zoning change.

Then things just started falling perfectly into place. Just

after we finalized the contract with Kerasotes, Nick Saraceno, a commercial real estate broker from Kritt Realty, brought us a potential buyer for the 25-acre parcel west of Central Avenue. Gerard Kenny, the chairman of the Chicagoland Laborers' District Council, was looking for a location for their new training facility. They already had a facility in Carol Stream, but they wanted another location closer to the city. This would allow them to provide better services to the inner-city population. There were few sites on the north side that could fulfill their needs. Galewood Yards became an ideal location for their training facility.

1900 N. Central Avenue: Galewood Yards included an AMC Showplace 14-screen theater, 190 units of residential housing (single-family and two-flats) and the Laborers' Union Training Center.

The mayor and the planning department got word that Mr. Kenny was interested in 25 acres at Galewood Yards. Now, this was a project that they could support; after years of struggle, we were able to get an agreement from the planning department to get the zoning we needed on the remaining land. We agreed to sell the 25-acre parcel to the Laborers' District Council at our cost, and the city agreed to support mixed-use zoning on the rest of the property. There could not have been a better arrangement. We were pleased to finally get the zoning issue behind us and gladly agreed to their proposal.

Our petition for zoning floated smoothly through the zoning committee, and was passed at a meeting in March 2006. With the zoning in place, we knew that we wouldn't have any problems selling the last parcel. We immediately closed on the deal with Kerasotes. They went right to work building a fourteen-screen movie complex, which was completed within one year. Around August 2006, we sold the final parcel to Red Seal Development for a residential planned unit development. Our investment in Galewood Yards proved to be very successful for our partnership. We repaid our investors' capital, along with a nice return on investment.

The partnership that was created for the purchase of the property was disbanded. But the story doesn't end there.

My partner, Bob Finnigan, and I both decided to invest $1.25 million each in the Red Seal Development project at Galewood Yards. The development was known as the Enclave at Galewood Yards. It included a total of 190 single-family homes, townhomes, and condominiums, priced from $199,000 to $399,000. These were very reasonable prices for homes in this part of the city. The residential real estate market was on fire. We believed the affordability of these homes ensured success, even in a market that appeared to be peaking. The project started off great by pre-selling 150 units from February to May 2007. However, by the time the homes were ready to close in 2008, the real estate market had started to considerably slow down. Only about 100 of the 150 units closed.

1900 N. Laramie Avenue: Two-flats at the Enclave of Galewood Yards.

We sold our partnership interest back to Red Seal Development at a loss of $2.4 million, and gave up all future rights to profits. We also wanted a release of liability on the project's debt obligation with J.P. Morgan Chase. But when we originally formed the partnership, we had given J.P. Morgan Chase our personal guarantees for the project's financing. J.P. Morgan Chase would not release us from liability.

I then proposed that Finnigan and I could purchase the remaining vacant lots in the Enclave development for $4.5 million. The money from the sale of the lots could go directly to paying off a portion of the debt. We would then be released from liability and Red Seal Development would be solely responsible for the remaining balance.

J.P. Morgan Chase agreed to my proposal, and Bob and I divested our interest in our partnership with Red Seal Development. Today, we still own fifteen lots in the development. The other half were sold at a discount to another real estate investor. The lots have lost almost 75% of their value since the crash of the real estate market. Through our partnership with Red Seal Development, we lost far more money than we had made from our original partnership, which had sold the land to them. If only this were the end of the story.

In August 2007, while we were still involved in the partnership with Red Seal at Galewood Yards, I discovered that I was the subject of a federal investigation. This came as a surprise. I didn't know what I had done to warrant any interest. Through my attorney, it was determined that the investigation was based on my involvement with a Chicago alderman, Isaac Carothers. Seventy percent of the property at Galewood Yards fell within the jurisdiction of Alderman Carothers' ward, and it was thought that I had bribed Alderman Carothers to obtain the zoning at Galewood Yards. When my attorney told me this, I felt as if my heart had just stopped beating. It took me a few minutes to gather my composure, as I then explained to him exactly what had happened.

On June 8, 2004, I received a call from Alderman Carothers. I had known him for some time; he was very active in the community and had voted on the zoning of other projects that I had developed in the city. He requested a referral for a general contractor to do some work at his personal residence. At the time, I didn't think anything of his request. People would contact me all the time looking for good contractors, recognizing that in my line of business, I had the opportunity to evaluate many general contractors. Familiar with Stanley Walczak's work and price, I suggested that the alderman contact him.

Stanley was a local non-union contractor that my company used frequently for smaller projects. I felt perfectly comfortable recommending Stanley to Alderman Carothers. I arranged a meeting and a few days later, I accompanied Stanley to the home of Alderman Carothers. After introducing the two men, I left them to discuss the work that needed to be done. As I was leaving, I didn't think there was anything wrong with the situation. I was happy that I was able to send some business Stanley's way, as well as pleased to be able to help Alderman Carothers find a reliable contractor.

A few weeks later, I received a call from Stanley. He sounded very anxious: "I am $37,000 into this project for Alderman Carothers, and now he wants new cabinets. I think that he thinks that one of us is paying for this project!" I calmly instructed Stanley to inform Alderman Carothers that his current cabinets were fine, and to wrap up the project, and to get out of there.

I felt responsible for getting Stanley involved in this mess. I had no idea that it would turn out this way. Alderman Carothers never said anything, directly or indirectly, about my paying for this project. We only discussed the fact that he had some work he needed done, and whether I could refer a reliable contractor to him. I was put in a very difficult situation. In all my years of business in Chicago, I had never experienced anything like this.

I figured I had only a few options. I could call Alderman Carothers and try to clear up the confusion, although I didn't want to risk alienating an alderman who could influence a zoning decision for my potential future development in his ward. Not only did I have capital at risk, but I had investors' capital at risk in this project, and I didn't want to jeopardize it. This option was problematic.

Alternatively, I could have just sent him an invoice and waited to see how he responded. In hindsight, this would have been my best option.

Instead, I chose to quietly pay Stanley for the work he completed, and hoped that this transaction never came back to haunt me. I will remember this decision for the rest of my life. It was the biggest mistake in my over 30-year career as a real estate developer.

As a result, I was indicted on May 30, 2009, about a week before the expiration of the statute of limitations.

* * * * *

On June 1st, my attorney accompanied me to the Chicago Federal Building, where I promptly posted a $500,000 cash bond and was released. It didn't take long; there was soon a flood of media coverage. I was already being tried in the press, even though my trial had not even started. People in Chicago believed that politicians, along with those who had dealings with them, were all corrupt. I knew that if I wanted a chance at winning this case that I would need the best trial attorney. I dismissed my attorney and hired Tom Mesereau and Robert Sanger. They were the legal team, from California, that handled Michael Jackson's criminal trial.

In March of 2010, I found myself on trial in federal court in the Northern District of Illinois. I was facing charges of one count of campaign violations for my involvement with Alderman Carothers and two counts of obstruction of justice.

I paid a seven-figure amount for my defense, but it didn't really make a difference. I was found guilty and sentenced to 46 months in federal prison. Alderman Carothers, on the other hand, negotiated a plea agreement in exchange for his cooperation with my case, and he received approximately a 26 month sentence.

We experienced great opposition from Mayor Daley and the City of Chicago Planning Department for over four years before we could reach an agreement on the zoning. I submit for your consideration, that Galewood Yards is a quality development for the community. It is now home to a 14-screen Kerasotes theater, affordable residential homes in the Enclave, and a world-class training facility for the Laborers' District Council. In defending Galewood Yards as a quality development for the community and my investors, I do not expect to justify my action with Alderman Carothers. I choose my behavior and society chooses my consequences. I must be accountable for my actions each moment of my life, or I am nothing to myself or society.

Summary

Really, It Pays to Read

I know I have already mentioned this once before, but it is so important that it is worth mentioning again: it pays to read. Reading about CMC Heartland selling land to Metra Rail, which was contiguous to the land we had under contract for $1 more per square foot, was fortuitous. We were able to renegotiate our contract and save our partnership $2 million at the closing table. I can never stress enough the value of staying informed of what is going on, not just at the local level, but also across the United States and abroad. Continuous reading will help a businessman generate new ideas and find ways to save money for his company.

Beware of Political Pitfalls

In Chicago, no single alderman has the absolute authority to grant zoning to a developer. The zoning process is very involved and requires the approval of numerous individuals at every step along the way, from the community level all the way to the city council. I believed that the vision the mayor and the planning commission shared for the Galewood Yards property was fundamentally flawed. It did not matter to them how untenable their position was. They had no money invested in the deal, so they weren't concerned that the land remained vacant for years while they searched for the perfect manufacturing tenant. The only advice I can give is to be sure to test the waters before venturing into any deal that could be politically charged. If a project does not line up with political interests, it simply is not going to happen. We tried to show the mayor the absurdity of the city's position on our property, but for years he wouldn't listen. Eventually, we came to a compromise, and Mayor Daley agreed to support our proposal in exchange for the sale of a parcel of our land to the Laborers' District Council at cost. I would have avoided this deal altogether, had I known it was going to be so politically volatile.

The End Does Not Justify the Means

Ultimately, it was Mayor Daley who got the zoning approved for Galewood Yards. I, however, formed an unholy alliance with Alderman Carothers because I feared what he could do to prevent the zoning from getting approved. In the end, the site was transformed into three quality developments: Kerasotes movie complex, Chicagoland Laborers' District Council training facility, and single-family townhomes and condominiums in the Enclave. The deal was profitable for all of the original investors in the partnership that purchased Galewood Yards. The project was a success, but I should have never made the inappropriate contributions to Alderman Carothers in the form of renovations to his home. It was a lapse in judgment. No matter how beneficial an outcome may be, the end never justifies the means if you have to sacrifice propriety to attain it. The dynamics of Galewood Yards may be my most important lesson in what an ethical man might do to gain the correct project for the community and his investors. It was easy to rationalize, but illegal by law.

Part II: Epilogue

Timing is Everything:
Historical Cycles

The Power of Quality Thought:
Future Trends

Timing Is Everything

Historical Cycles

I learned a valuable lesson in my 30 years of business: a businessman, no matter how great or small, must float along with the waves of growth. From 1979 to 1990, without knowing, I obeyed this natural law of business. In the early 1990s, however, while America was in a recession, I pushed into suburban real estate and failed. I realized that I was not the sole power driving my financial success. The economic cycles were, in fact, absolutely in control. If my goal was continued success, I recognized that I should never try to flow against these cycles. Since then, I have made understanding the underlying historical cycles in the marketplace an essential aspect in my business decisions.

When economies are in depression, much like what began in 2008, all of the value of mediocre to good real estate projects is reduced. The mediocre projects depress to the point of having no return on equity or a negative value, and the better quality projects reduce from having a high return on equity to an average rate of return. Such was the case with the parking garage that Bob Finnigan and I owned, at the corner of Washington and Franklin Streets in downtown Chicago.

Our garage was built in 1999, and it quickly became the best asset we owned. Within 3 days of opening, it was full. The garage provided a 20% return for the $6.5 million in investor equity we brought to the deal. From 2000 to 2010, Bob Finnigan and I each received over $3 million in cash flow from the garage. In the economy we experienced in 2012, the garage was only paying a 10% return to the partners. We saw our income cut by half.

The garage is still a good asset compared to most real estate. Most real estate is average, and the depression has yet to complete its destruction of commercial and residential real estate values.

A top-quality asset will survive a downturn in the economy better than a lesser quality asset. Thus, an investor in real estate should try to buy properties in the best locations. Owning an apartment building near a college, having property close to a stable job market, or possessing commercial space on the best retail corners in a town, are all means by which a real estate investor can protect himself against negative changes in market conditions.

The following chart shows the Case-Shiller Index of home prices from 1890 to 2010. Looking at the chart, we see that home values, adjusted for inflation, were actually higher in 1890 than for most of the following 50 years, even with the unprecedented growth the U.S. experienced from 1880 to 1920.

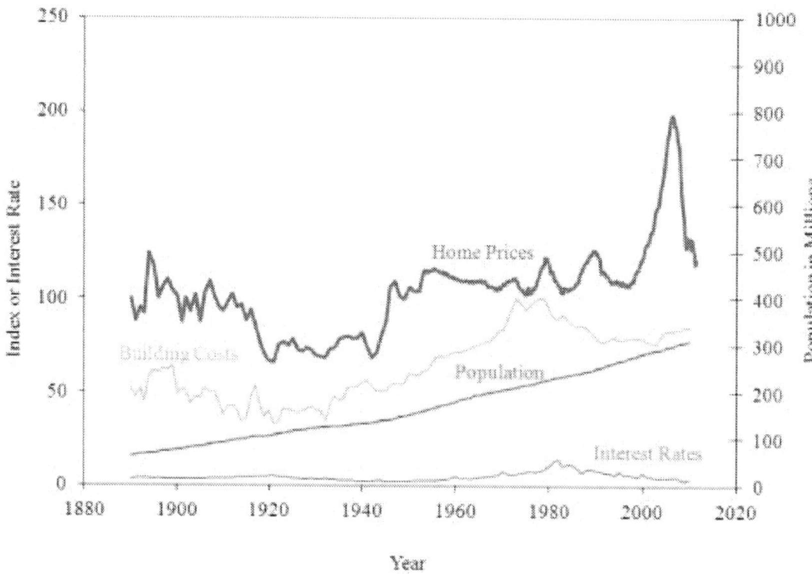

The technological advances, such as the telephone, automobile, and the light bulb, transformed culture, invented the modern city, and had a positive effect on home values. From 1910 to 1920, as the benefits of the new technology diminished, the prices and values of homes gradually declined. Prices then remained relatively stable until 1943, when Americans believed the end of World War II was in sight, and once again, values increased. With no major technological advances from 1943 to 1955, the prices again remained relatively stable.

By the late 1990s, the commercialization of the Internet and the advances in personal computer technology had a major impact on our culture. These technologies were completely discounted into the economy by the mid 2000s. Additionally, since 2001, there has been nothing but uncertainty caused by the United States' military involvement overseas. There must have been other factors at play, then, that influenced the real estate boom that peaked in 2007. Had the increase in home values been attributed to a major technological breakthrough or world peace, it may have been sustainable. Such was not the case.

In 1994, the Clinton administration and other elected officials decided that more Americans should be homeowners. At the time, 64% of Americans already owned their own home. This figure had remained relatively consistent since the 1950s. Nevertheless, President Clinton believed that the American Dream should be available to all Americans. It would have been very unrealistic to shoot for 100% homeownership; they were aiming to increase the rate to 70%. Our elected leaders began a campaign, along with two government-sponsored enterprises that purchased consumer mortgages in the secondary market, Fannie Mae and Freddie Mac, to encourage more Americans to become homeowners.

Fannie Mae and Freddie Mac were two quasi-governmental agencies that liberalized their underwriting standards to broaden the availability of financing a home to more people. Americans with lower credit scores and less income could buy not only the home they felt they needed, but possibly a bigger and more expensive home than they could rationally afford. Such wonderful mortgage products as the 20% down, no-documentation loan, allowed parents to put a down payment on a nice home for their child, with the promise that the child would make the monthly payments. Of course, the home was generally too much home for this first-time home buyer, and these properties inevitably went into foreclosure. Parents had the 20% down payment, but could not afford to pay all the bills when they found out that their child did not have the income for the mortgage, taxes, maintenance, and all of the other expenses that go along with owning a home. These loans became known in the industry as "20% Down Liar Loans." If a borrower had 20% down, no documentation of income was required; therefore, the borrower could just lie about the extent of their income. Products like this, and other predatory lending practices, were the undoing of the mortgage industry.

Fannie Mae and Freddie Mac now hold up to 30% of all home mortgages in America. They buy billions of dollars in loans from mortgage companies and banks that just want to earn a fee for originating the loan and sell the risk of holding the loan to one of these two companies that have implied government backing. As one may guess, once our elected officials got the great idea of increasing the rate of homeownership in America, it was going to happen. Anyone who tried to suggest that it was a bad idea was labeled as "anti-American." Since this experiment has gone severely wrong, the government has been forced to inject cash into both Fannie Mae and Freddie Mac to keep them afloat. When the dust settles, the United States government will be the proud owner of millions of homes.

The loosening up of loan application standards created the first punch of a one-two-punch scenario. The second came in 2003, when then Chairman of the Federal Reserve Board, Alan Greenspan, saw the economy lingering in a recessionary environment. Over the course of one year, Greenspan reduced the Federal Funds rate, the rate at which the Federal Reserve Bank loans money to other banks, from 6% down to 1%. With the new Federal Funds rate at 1%, mortgage companies and banks could offer mortgages with interest rates of 4% to 5% for a fixed term. If a borrower had good credit and wanted an adjustable-rate or floating-rate mortgage, these types of products were available with rates starting as low as 1.75%, just .75% over the Federal Funds lending rate.

In a conversation I had with Brian Hoffman, a fellow real estate developer, I asked him what he thought of Greenspan lowering interest rates to 1%. He responded, "These low interest rates will be like crack cocaine to people financing a home. They will make the market surge. The growth will all be an illusion that is not sustainable, and it will all end badly." I agreed with Hoffman.

As we predicted, the combination of low interest rates and the relaxed lending practices put both the real estate and corporate markets on a tear. Cheap money flowed everywhere. Businesses and consumers frantically bought up assets, which turned out to be overvalued, in an attempt to take advantage of the low interest rates. Many consumers purchased homes using adjustable-rate mortgages with low initial rates. This allowed home buyers to borrow a greater amount of money at the lowest possible rates, resulting in a monthly payment they could afford. This was a recipe for disaster. It would only take a rise in interest rates or a decrease in income to put strain on a homeowner's ability to make his mortgage payment. Homeowners were so happy to be living the American Dream, they were not even aware of how precarious their position really was.

Greenspan retired in 2006, and Ben Bernanke took over as the new chairman of the Federal Reserve Board. He was then responsible for the financial train wreck Greenspan had created. By 2011, three years after the real estate market crash of 2008, American income was declining and inflation was, and still is, rampant. By 2012, the country has amassed over $16 trillion in debt and continues to devalue the dollar by printing currency. The United States has lost its universal

AAA credit rating. When interest rates are at zero, they can only move up, which will eventually happen when foreigners and Treasury bond holders around the world are no longer willing to accept the low interest rates invented by Greenspan in 2003, and taken to near zero by Bernanke.

These higher interest rates will further devalue real estate, as higher mortgage payments will create another massive round of foreclosures in America. When this happens, the buyers of real estate will buy at a much lower value because this will be all they can afford. Just as lower interest rates artificially inflated property values from 2003 to 2008, now higher interest rates will devalue real estate as never before. Property values will eventually return to the average levels where they have been historically sustainable. When the real estate market returns to sustainable levels, the spike in real estate prices experienced in the 2000s will come to be viewed as a nonsensical journey bordering on delusional thinking on the part of our central bank.

Following major historical price trends through market cycles can add value. Buying a property in 1984 would have been a good move. The economy was experiencing a recession in the early 1980s, and by 1985, conditions were starting to improve. Buying in 1994 would have provided the same up-side potential. Following the 2008 recession to its bottom would offer the same business advantages as 1984 and 1994. Many think that we had already reached the bottom in 2013, but that is not true. As consumer mortgage interest rates return to their historical norm of 6% to 8%, property values will further decline. We may not reach the bottom for several years. Real estate most likely will bounce along the bottom for several years. Do not expect another fast moving economy to raise values quickly. We need deflation to bring the prices of real estate, stocks, and other assets back to sustainable pre-1998 levels. By 2012, home values had already been reduced to 2002 levels, and this deflationary process must continue.

Our government is currently trying to postpone the pain of deflation by printing money to buy back United States Treasury bonds. As of 2012, of the more than $16 trillion in bonds, 17% of all bonds are owned by the Federal Reserve. This is not good. Imagine a shoe maker who buys all of his own shoes. Of course, he is not going to be in business very long. The same is true for the United States. Through the process of what the Federal Reserve refers to as quantitative easing, they have monetized a portion of our debt by buying back Treasury bonds. This process may continue if Bernanke decides on a third round of quantitative easing. The sooner our government stops buying its own bonds back, the sooner interest rates can resume their normal course. Only then, can the American economy begin its recovery.

As of 2013, America has become a part of an inevitable perfect storm of deflation, which is shrinking the economy. There are many factors that are driving this deflationary force. Keeping the Federal Funds rate low only provides a false market stimulus and slows the unavoidable deflation which needs to occur. The current practice by the Federal Reserve of buying back our Treasury bonds as fast as we print them, will not change the mega-deflationary trend we are experiencing. The deflation in real estate, stocks, and other assets is larger than any central bank can fix. They are fighting a losing battle.

The Federal Reserve Bank was not created until 1913. Its first chairman was J.P. Morgan. Morgan knew enough to allow deflation to occur naturally in the economy. Today, our economy is seeing its largest productive employee base, the Baby Boomers, reach their mid-sixties and begin to retire. The Baby Boomer generation has 76 million people. The next generation after them, Generation X is only 35 million strong, and will never have the same impact on the economy as the Baby Boomers. Generation X is just now in its productive years. This reduced number of productive employees in the workforce is contributing to the deflationary pressure in the economy. It is a problem much bigger than the Federal Reserve can remedy. Once the next generation, the Echo Boomers (millennials), enters the workforce and become productive members of society, their energy will help drive the recovery.

Echo Boomers are the children of Baby Boomers. There are about 92 million Echo Boomers, some of which have already graduated from college, and are beginning to enter the workforce. This generation will drive demand for everything from housing to automobiles. These individuals are the ones who will live through the next big technological breakthroughs. The technology of the Internet, personal computer, and cell phone energized the years from 1985 to 2003 just like the automobile, telephone, and electric light bulb did from 1890 to 1910. These two waves of technology, 100 years apart, created unthinkable economic growth for America. We need new technologies to drive the next stage of economic growth.

The development of advanced battery technology that would allow the storage of solar energy during the day for use at night, or that would permit an electric car to travel 300 miles on one charge, could be the impetus the economy needs. Maybe technology that increases crop yields and makes food more affordable, or technologies such as wind and solar, which decrease our dependence on foreign oil, will be the solution. There are so many breakthroughs that could revolutionize our daily lives. The Echo Boomers are in a position to solve some of these problems and, in the process, help drive the economy to future growth.

The shame of our central bank throwing trillions of dollars into currency and trying to stop the current deflation is, in effect, destroying the equity of all Americans. Whether it is cash in the bank, real estate assets, or stocks, the reckless increasing of the money supply is diminishing the overall equity of all citizens. The debt that the Federal Reserve is creating is our debt, and as of August 2012, it has affected our credit rating as a country. The lowering of our credit rating, by one credit rating agency, is a signal that the United States is more likely to default on its debt obligations than before.

The United States government will continue to send out the Social Security checks and they will continue to honor its Treasury bonds, but the radical increase in the money supply in itself will be a default. The Social Security checks will fall short of their ability to provide the necessities for our retirees, and the real value of the Treasury bonds when they are paid off may be 30% to 50% less than the value the holder of the bond may think it has. Technically speaking, this will not be seen as a default, but the damage to Social Security recipients and foreign debt holders will be substantial.

If the current deflation finds a bottom in 2013 or 2014, then assets will be positioned for a new movement up in the economy. For this upward movement to happen, the Echo Boomers must be engaged in a growing, vital workforce, and must find the next wave of technology to help move our economy in the right direction. The intersection of Echo Boomer population growth, new technology, lower energy costs, and low asset values will be the catalyst for dynamic growth. This new economy will start slowly in 2015 and be engaging all Americans by 2020.

Investors, whether in real estate or other assets, need to be aware of the market cycles and their effect on the economy. Our businesses do not exist in a vacuum. There are always both microeconomic and macroeconomic factors that can have an impact on an investment. Understanding the relationships between the ebb and flow of a market cycle and a specific investment, is very important to the success of that investment. An investor has to always remain informed—not just about his local economy, but also, even more so now, about the global economy.

The Power of Quality Thought

Future Trends

No one really knows what the future holds for those engaged in real estate or those involved in business in general. I have taken notice of trends that have developed over the years that continue to evolve. In order for our economy to recover from our current recession, certain behaviors do need to change. Poor tax policy and government control of interest rates are not the solution to our nation's problems. The following analyses cover trends that I see advancing, or present trends that need to advance. Not all of these trends will be beneficial to business in the future in the United States. We need to be able to identify these trends before they come fully to fruition, and are detrimental to economic growth.

Trends in Real Estate Valuation

Today, we are watching the crazy housing valuations of 2007 decline into what will eventually become an overcorrection. It may be several years before prices reach their bottom. Given the surplus of housing in 2013, communities have resorted to devising radical solutions to deal with the vacant properties that litter their neighborhoods. I envision a drastic measure, taken in Chicago in the 1970s, reoccurring in the present time: vacant lots offered for $1.00.

In the 1970s, Cook County, Illinois, had hundreds of vacant lots that had been abandoned by their owners scattered throughout the city of Chicago. These lots were an inconvenience for the city. No one was paying the real estate taxes on the property or maintaining them.

The lots were overgrown with weeds and inundated with garbage. The city decided to offer the vacant lots to any homeowner owning property adjacent to one of the lots for $1.00. In exchange, the new owner would be responsible to keep the lot clean and to pay the real estate taxes.

Unfortunately, very few people took advantage of this offer. Owning more Chicago real estate may have been the last thing on their minds. A lot of people were just trying to survive with what they already had. Of course, 30 years later, many of these lots each have become worth $500,000 to $1 million.

Local governments rely on the income generated through real estate taxes. The wave of foreclosures throughout the country has put stress on the budgets of many local municipalities. These governments will have to be creative to attract buyers of the vacant properties in their communities. Tax sales that offer a property for sale in return for the payment of back taxes may not be successful. We then may again see homes sold or offered for $1.00. Local governments will be content with simply having someone pay the real estate taxes going forward.

At first glance, homes for $1.00 might sound like a great investment opportunity. This will be a great opportunity for people who have the determination and equity to fix up a home to live in for themselves. In reality, most investors will not buy these properties as rental units because there will be a shortage of tenants. In many communities across the United States, there is a surplus of housing and a shortage of jobs. Young adults are continuing to live at home with their parents, and retirees are being forced to move in with their children, further suppressing demand in the housing market. An investor needs to carefully conduct a cost-benefit analysis to determine if a buy and hold strategy would be appropriate for a property in a specific market.

This surplus of housing may well be the biggest problem affecting valuations in many markets. I foresee some subdivisions being bulldozed. The lenders, who own all of these properties through foreclosure, and local communities will see no demand to live in certain areas. They will consider demolition the best way to relinquish their need to maintain these properties and to prevent vandalism. Reducing the supply of housing will increase home values, but this is not something that will happen overnight. It could take years for property values to bounce back. When this recovery occurs, an investor who now has the wherewithal to pay repair costs, maintenance, and real estate taxes out of his own pocket while a property generates no cash flow, could be positioned well to benefit accordingly.

Trends in Taxation

Strapped for cash, the federal government, along with many state and local governments, are trying to formulate new ways to generate more income. Recently, a trend has developed, increasing taxation across the board on individuals, corporations, and assets. It seems that government taxing authorities believe that the most successful businesses and people should be the target for their new tax initiatives. I would not have a problem paying more taxes, up to a point, if I knew that government would spend my tax dollars responsibly. It amazes me how I have become increasingly convinced of this trend more every year, as I watched my parking garage become subjected to more and more city and county taxes.

The Washington Franklin Self-Park operation, previously owned by my company, took in between $4 million and $4.5 million per year. The Cook County real estate taxes were $820,000 in 2010, and there were separate City of Chicago and Cook County parking taxes, adding another $900,000 in expenses. In October 2011, new Chicago Mayor Rahm Emanuel suggested another tax on downtown parking garages as a means of helping to overcome the city's $659 million budget deficit. If you do the math, without accounting for any new taxes, approximately 40% of the income from my parking garage goes towards some form of government taxes before the federal government has a chance to get their hands in the pot. Essentially, a fiscally irresponsible local government raises taxes on an entity, which results in more taxes being paid overall, but now the federal government gets a smaller slice of the pie. For now, the federal government allows a deduction for state and local taxes in determining an entity's taxable income. If state and local governments continue to erode the federal government's tax base, these deductions may soon be modified.

Fortunately, my parking garage did not carry a lot of debt, and it still managed to provide decent cash flow to its investors. The question is: how much more taxation will it take to completely sap all cash flow?

In the early 1990s, I ran across an interesting story in the *Chicago Tribune* about Amoco Oil Company and the effects of taxation on one of its domestic refineries. The article began by explaining how Hugo Chavez, the late president of Venezuela, had seized Amoco's assets in the country and nationalized the oil operations. The reporter asked an Amoco executive how they could justify spending so much money in Venezuela, only to have it all taken away. The executive gave an answer that was very telling of the future: he responded that Amoco had a refinery and oil storage facility in Whiting, Indiana, which was located in Lake County. The county taxed this facility until it reached the point where it was no longer profitable for the company to operate. The executive then further commented that Chavez took Amoco's assets with guns and power and sent them packing. He considered this a more honest approach than what had occurred in Lake County, Indiana, where government taxed the asset until it was destroyed. In Whiting, Amoco must still run the asset at no profit, but in Venezuela, at least they suffer no further.

Amoco is at the mercy of Lake County. They could not easily pick up and move their operation somewhere else. That is not true for all businesses, though. Taxing authorities, in implementing tax rates, must consider what taxes are in other areas of the country and across the world. Companies and creative minds, that are able to relocate, will vote with their feet. They will leave a state or a country that they feel is financially oppressive with high tax rates to move to a place that is more equitable. Companies are in business to provide a return to their investors. If a better return can be achieved in a different state or country, companies will pull up their roots and move.

Consider Caterpillar, for example, a company that conducts business across the globe. In 2011, when Caterpillar, headquartered in Peoria, Illinois, observed an increase in the state corporate tax rate from 7.3% to 9.5%, they notified the state that they were considering relocating. Caterpillar could move their corporate headquarters to another state, or even another country, with only a minor disruption to their income statement. Their business is not limited to Illinois. What incentive is there for Caterpillar to remain in the state?

In the future, states and other countries will be competing for successful companies and people. Taxing authorities falsely assume that people and businesses will not leave their geographical domain. The overtaxing by these authorities will destroy the wealth of employment, ideas, and capital that these companies bring to their communities. Areas that provide the best incentives will attract the best companies. It is that simple.

Trends in Lending

There are two sides to lending: consumer lending and commercial lending. Over the years, consumer lending had been a function of smaller local banks and credit unions. In the late 1980s, following the savings and loan crisis, many community banks and savings and loan operations went bankrupt. Over the next 10 to 15 years, smaller banks were acquired by larger regional banks. This left a void in the banking system. There are now fewer institutions whose primary focus is providing consumer banking services.

The larger commercial banks primarily make their money from business-to-business relationships. They usually offer services for consumers, but their emphasis is on their commercial lending operations. These are the banks like J.P. Morgan Chase, Citibank, and Bank of America. The corporate structure of these banks makes it next to impossible for them to ever have the feel of a local bank to a customer. Smaller banks have autonomy and follow the traditional approach to lending—the three C's: character, capacity, and collateral.

We will see a shift in trends as banks rely less on the current lending model, where a borrower's information is input into a computer to make a risk assessment, to the more personal three C's approach. As a result of the mortgage crisis in 2008, lenders have bolstered their underwriting standards to a point that only those with the best credit will qualify. But these are not the people who need help the most. A transition must occur in lending that will level the playing field for all borrowers by overlooking a person's credit history and focusing more on their character, capacity, and collateral.

Only smaller banks are capable of developing relationships with customers and be in a position to evaluate a borrower's character. In the fourth quarter of 2011, hoards of consumers switched from large national banks to smaller local banks and credit unions, as the big banks scrambled to find new ways to generate revenue through increased fees. The larger banks have alienated their customer bases. Small banks, as a result, have a chance to capture control of the consumer banking industry.

For local banks to again take control over consumer lending, interest rates have to go up. These banks will have to rely on Tier 1 capital to finance their lending operations. Artificially low interest rates hurt savers who want to invest in money market accounts and certificates of deposits. These types of investments are very attractive to people looking for a safe return on their money. Savers need to be able to get 4%

to 5% return just to stay ahead of inflation. If interest rates rise to sufficiently allow neighborhood banks to offer favorable returns to our older generation of savers and, in turn, allow the banks to have the necessary capital to finance consumer loans for our younger generation of borrowers, consumer loans should prosper. This would be the true essence of saving and lending.

In giving the power of consumer lending back to the smaller consumer banks, the big banks will be able to focus more on their strength: commercial lending. Rising interest rates, which are necessary to encourage more saving, will be the last hindrance to economic recovery. Federal Reserve Chairman Ben Bernanke wants to keep the Federal Funds rate at or below 1%. With interest rates that low, there is no incentive to save. With Federal Funds rate at 1%, it only delays the inevitable rise in interest rates that has to occur for true recovery to happen. Banks need to be moved away from borrowing cheap Federal funds. If they had to rely on other capital to make loans, the marketplace, not the Federal Reserve, would dictate interest rates.

My first development project, Wrightwood Court Townhomes, was financed by Lakeview Bank in 1986. By 1990, I had developed a good relationship with my bankers at Lakeview when they were purchased by LaSalle Bank. That relationship continued at LaSalle, but I noticed the dynamics of the relationship changing. The bank I started doing business with had morphed from a small neighborhood bank into a behemoth organization, which had lost touch with the community. I had access to better interest rates, but they did not understand my business as well as my original bankers had at Lakeview Bank. This lack of understanding required me to jump through more hoops in order to obtain financing for projects. These restrictions are making it more and more difficult for people to get loans. Banks today are sitting on a lot of capital that could be used to make loans, but they are afraid to take a chance on borrowers in this economy. We need banks to shift to the more personal approach to lending to help spur the economy along the road to recovery.

Being aware of the trends in business and the economy can help an investor make strategic decisions to stay ahead of a trend. The ability to recognize the trends in housing valuation, taxation, and lending are crucial in real estate. Housing in some areas will reach very inexpensive levels as taxing authorities look for ways to generate more revenue. Taxing authorities that implement new taxes during the recession are not very likely to withdraw them during a recovery. In addition, lending must still become more personal. Once this happens and a recovery begins, housing valuations will rise. The good news is that until banking becomes more personal, there may be opportunities for creative financing solutions through options like owner financing, where a homeowner needs to sell a house, but the buyer cannot get financing. Trends such as this could help or hurt the economy in the coming years—it will be interesting and insightful to witness and live it.

Postlude

In telling the story of my career in real estate development, I wanted to give you, the reader, the good and the bad. This book is in no way comprehensive of all the deals I have ever done. There were many stories that were omitted because frankly, they were not very exciting, or they bordered on being redundant. I recounted important and meaningful transactions that had great impact on me as well as details of situations that could provide other business professionals with knowledge of how certain situations, whether or not expected, could happen to them if they are not careful. I never thought Galewood Yards could happen to me. However, it did, and it put me where I am today.

In ancient times, the Romans had a celebration when their armies returned from war. The centurions would ride in chariots into the amphitheater in full dress uniform to the applause of the adoring citizenry. On the shoulder of each centurion was placed a little bird. This bird's duty was to whisper in the ear of each centurion that all fame and fortune is fleeting and to stay on guard lest you fail.

If you are not proactive at all times, about both business and political relationships, you can back yourself into unethical situations and be compromised by your circumstances. I was not proactive enough in the summer of 2004. My decision to pay for the renovations on Alderman Carothers' home was a major mistake. On a different day—and I would like to think on every other day—I could have made an entirely different decision. I was at the pinnacle of my career and distracted by my success. My wife had just thrown a 50th birthday party for me at the Adler Planetarium in Chicago, which featured dinner with 240 of my friends, family, and business associates, along with live entertainment from The Temptations. Life could not get any better. I was relaxed and mentally taking a break from my business obligations. Of course, this is in no way a defense of the decision I made. Like the centurions of old, in the summer of 2004, I needed one of those birds from the Roman celebration whispering in my ear. I let my guard down. I take full responsibility for my actions.

Author's Postscript

I am currently reading a book first published in 1947. In its "About the Author Section", the author describes himself as a physician, printer, reporter, editor, soldier and photographer. His description made me smile because, today, conventional wisdom is that everyone should focus like a laser on one career path - or else you'll be a jack of all trades but a master of none. On the surface, I have invested 32 years of my life into the real estate industry and, in a sense, this single-minded focus is largely responsible for my success.

However, in my college years, I worked as a carpenter and drove a garbage truck through the streets of Chicago. Unknown to me then, I was learning valuable lessons that I have applied later in my real estate career. Working as a carpenter helped me understand construction, the costs of bringing labor and materials to a project, and completing the project on a specific budget. In the early 1970s, my experience as a "Garbio", as garbage truck drivers in Chicago were called, helped me to understand Chicago's streets and neighborhoods, when they were much rougher than today. My skills as a carpenter and a Garbio were no better than the other guys, but the **experience** I gained served as a base of knowledge for my future success. Through my experience as a carpenter, one of the many things I learned was that 55 cents of every dollar spent on real estate development was for hard construction. Understanding construction costs and how they affected project budgets was pivotal to my success as a real estate developer. Driving a garbage truck was not about becoming a great Garbio, it was really about learning and becoming comfortable in the dilapidated streets of an urban market ready to explode with development opportunities.

My motto is "always look both ways on a one-way street". Unknowingly, we all learn from our everyday experiences. We can use that knowledge to take advantage of opportunity when it presents itself. Be open to opportunity when it comes along – or it will pass us by in an instant! By looking both ways on life's one-way street and remaining cognizant of our experiences, we will be fully prepared to jump when the opportunity presents itself.

Throughout my career, I was fortunate enough to draw on a wide array of experiences and my rich background when making key decisions and building my business. Think about how you, too, can become a "jack" of a few new trades as you review the ideas and concepts set forth in this book. It isn't important whether you agree or disagree with my observations – what is truly important is that we all remain open to new ideas, the next great challenge, and upcoming opportunities. In that spirit, being a jack of all trades makes me, and probably you, a lot more like the author from 1947 then we realize!

INDEX

About the Author

Calvin Boender resides in the suburbs of Chicago with his wife, son and 2 dogs. He is currently focusing on developing solutions to future challenges of the agricultural real estate market.